P9-DXI-499

ONE NATION

ONE NATION

—

WHAT WE CAN ALL DO TO
SAVE AMERICA'S FUTURE

BEN CARSON, MD,
WITH CANDY CARSON

SENTINEL

SENTINEL
Published by the Penguin Group
Penguin Group (USA) LLC
375 Hudson Street
New York, New York 10014

USA | Canada | UK | Ireland | Australia | New Zealand | India | South Africa | China
penguin.com
A Penguin Random House Company

First published by Sentinel, a member of Penguin Group (USA) LLC, 2014

ISBN 978-1-59523-112-3

Printed in the United States of America
3   5   7   9   10   8   6   4

Set in Garamond MT Std
Designed by Alissa Rose Theodor

Dedicated to the millions of Americans who fought, sacrificed, and died to provide freedom and prosperity for us and our progeny.

CONTENTS

—

CONTENTS

PREFACE

THE 2013 NATIONAL PRAYER BREAKFAST

I was totally shocked when in the fall of 2012 my office received a call inquiring whether I would be willing to give the keynote address for the 2013 National Prayer Breakfast. I had already had the pleasure and honor of being the keynote speaker for the 1997 National Prayer Breakfast when President Clinton was in office. That speech was well received, even by President Clinton, despite my pointed comments about integrity in public office. "I just want to know who is responsible for putting this guy on before me," he quipped when he came to the podium after my talk. The audience roared with laughter and he went on to give his usual very good speech. The event had gone as well as it could have, but I didn't give a second thought as to whether I'd be asked again.

Stunned by the request, I asked if anyone had ever done it twice and I was informed that only one person fit into that category and that was Billy Graham. I prayed about it and felt that there was a reason why I was being asked for a repeat performance. I talked by telephone and in person with members of the National Prayer Breakfast staff and they informed me that many senators thought that I was the right person not only to encourage people but also to help bring a sense of unity back to our nation's capital. I was honored to accept the challenge and immediately begin praying for the necessary wisdom and words to gently address the spiritual, financial, and moral decline of America, a difficult task in the highly partisan atmosphere that exists in Washington, DC, today.

The event organizers were obviously familiar with many of my public speeches in which I had taken no prisoners. I call it as I see it without dancing around a topic in order to spare everyone's feelings. They were therefore somewhat concerned that I might say something that would offend the president. I indicated that I had no intention of offending anyone, the president included. Nevertheless, the organizers were still quite interested in receiving a copy of my transcript just to be on the safe side. I informed them that the 1997 National Prayer Breakfast committee had also wanted a copy of my notes but because I don't speak from a transcript, I wasn't able to provide them with a copy at that time either.

The breakfast was held at the Washington Hilton in the District of Columbia. The predictable protocols were shared by security and the Secret Service the evening before the event. And in the morning, I had the opportunity to chat with other participants in the Green Room over breakfast appetizers. I recalled that the menu in 1997 was considerably more varied and robust, and thinking that the fact that the selections were meager was a good thing since the federal budget is under a lot of pressure. I also remember the affability of the president and first lady in the 1997 receiving line. They were both very gracious and easy to talk to. This year, President and Mrs. Obama were not present in the Green Room, so there really was no opportunity to meet them or chat beforehand. However, there were many well-known dignitaries in the platform party there. Once we were on stage, I was seated on one side of the podium between Vice President Biden and Senator Schumer of New York, while the president was seated on the other side of the lectern between his wife and Senator Sessions of Alabama.

Before my speech, Bible readings and inspirational comments were made by a variety of people. I was introduced, followed by very generous applause, and began my speech by reading several Bible verses that seemed particularly applicable to the leadership in Washington, DC, today. The text of the speech follows:

Thank you so much. Mr. President, Mr. Vice President, Mrs. Obama, and distinguished guests . . . which includes everybody. Thank you so much for this wonderful honor to be at this stage again. I was here 16 years ago, and the fact that they invited me back means that I didn't offend too many people, so that was great.

I want to start by reading four texts which will put into context what I'm going to say.

Proverbs 11:9: Evil words destroy one's friends; wise discernment rescues the godly.

Proverbs 11:12: It is foolish to belittle a neighbor; a person with good sense remains silent.

Proverbs 11:25: The generous prosper and are satisfied; those who refresh others will themselves be refreshed.

2 Chronicles 7:14: Then if my people who are called by my name will humble themselves and pray and seek my face and turn from their wicked ways, I will hear from heaven and will forgive their sins and heal their land.

You know, I have an opportunity to speak in a lot of venues. This is my fourth speech this week. And I have an opportunity to talk to a lot of people. And I've been asking people what concerns you? What are you most concerned about in terms of the spirituality and the direction of our nation and our world? I've talked to very prominent Democrats . . . very prominent Republicans. And I was surprised by the uniformity of their answers. And those (answers) have informed my comments this morning.

Now, it's not my intention to offend anyone. I have discovered, however, in recent years that it's very difficult to speak to a large group of people these days and not offend someone. People walk around with their feelings on their shoulders waiting for you to say something. "Ah, did you hear that?" and they can't hear anything else you say. The PC police are out in force at all times. I remember once I was talking to a group about the difference between a human brain and a dog's brain, and a man got offended. He said, "You can't talk about dogs like that!" People just focus in on that . . . completely miss the point of what you're saying. And we've reached the point where people are afraid to actually talk about what they want to say because somebody might be offended. People are afraid to say "Merry Christmas" at Christmastime. Doesn't matter whether the person you're talking to is Jewish or, you know, whether they're any religion. That's a salutation, a greeting of goodwill. We've got to get over this sensitivity. You know it keeps people from saying what they really believe.

You know, I'm reminded of a very successful young businessman. And he loved to buy his mother these exotic gifts for Mother's Day. [One year] he ran out of ideas, and then he ran across these birds. These birds were cool, you know? They cost $5,000 apiece. They could dance, they could sing, they could talk! He was so excited, he bought two of them. Sent them to his mother, couldn't wait to call her up on Mother's Day, "Mother, Mother, what'd you think of those birds?" And she said, "They was good." [laughter] He said, "No, no, no! Mother, you didn't eat those birds? Those birds cost $5,000 apiece! They could dance, they could sing, they could talk!" And she said, "Well, they should have said something." [laughter] And, you know, that's where we'll end up, too, if we don't speak up for what we believe. [laughter] And, you know, what we need to do—[applause]what we need to do in this PC world is forget about unanimity of speech and unanimity of thought, and we need to concentrate on being respectful to those people with whom we disagree.

And that's when I think we begin to make real progress. And one last thing about political correctness, which I think is a horrible thing, by the way. I'm very, very compassionate, and I'm not ever out to offend anyone. But PC is dangerous. Because you see, in this country, one of the founding principles was freedom of thought and freedom of expression. And it muffles people. It puts a muzzle on them. And at the same time, keeps people from discussing important issues while the fabric of this society is being changed. And we cannot fall for that trick. And what we need to do is start talking about things . . . talking about things that are important. Things that were important in the development of our nation.

One of those things was education. I'm very passionate

about education because it made such a big difference in my life. But here we are at a time in the world—the information age, the age of technology—and yet 30% of people who enter high school in this country do not graduate. 44% of people who start a four-year college program do not finish it in four years. What is that about? Think back to a darker time in our history. Two hundred years ago when slavery was going on it was illegal to educate a slave, particularly to teach them to read. Why do you think that was? Because when you educate a man, you liberate a man. And there I was as a youngster placing myself in the same situation that a horrible institution did because I wasn't taking advantage of the education. I was a horrible student. Most of my classmates thought I was the stupidest person in the world. They called me "Dummy." I was the butt of all the jokes.

Now, admittedly, it was a bad environment. Single-parent home . . . you know my mother and father had gotten divorced early on. My mother got married when she was 13. She was one of 24 children. Had a horrible life. Discovered that her husband was a bigamist, had another family. And she only had a third-grade education. She had to take care of us. Dire poverty. I had a horrible temper and poor self-esteem. All the things that you think would preclude success. But I had something very important. I had a mother who believed in me. And I had a mother who would never allow herself to be a victim no matter what happened . . . never made excuses, and she never accepted an excuse from us. And if we ever came up with an excuse, she always said, "Do you have a brain?" And if the answer was yes, then she said, "Then you could have thought your way out of it." It doesn't matter what John or Susan or Mary or anybody else did or said. And it was the most important thing she did for my brother and myself. Because if you don't accept excuses, pretty soon people stop giving them, and they start looking for solutions. And that is a critical issue when it comes to success.

Well, you know, we did live in dire poverty. And one of the things that I hated was poverty. You know, some people hate spiders, some people hate snakes . . . I hated poverty. I couldn't stand it. [laughter] But, you know, my mother couldn't stand the fact that we were doing poorly in school. And she prayed and she asked God to give her wisdom . . . what could she do to get her young sons to understand the importance of developing their minds, so that they could control their own lives? And you know what, God gave her the wisdom . . . at least in her opinion. My brother and I didn't think it was that wise. Because it was to turn off the TV, let us watch only two or three TV programs during the week, and with all that spare time read two books apiece from the Detroit Public Libraries and submit to her written book reports which she couldn't read, but we didn't know that. She'd put check marks and highlights and stuff—but, you know I just hated this. And my friends were out having a good time. Her friends would criticize her. They would say, "You can't make boys stay in the house reading books, they'll grow up and they'll hate you." And I would overhear them and say, "Mother, you know they're right." But she didn't care, you know.

But, after a while, I actually began to enjoy reading those books, because we were very poor. But between the covers of those books I could go anywhere, I could be anybody, I could do anything. I began to read about people of great accomplishment. And as I read those stories, I began to see a connecting thread. I began to see that the person who has the most to do with you and what happens to you in life, is you. You make decisions. You decide how much energy you want to put behind that decision. And I came to understand that I had control of my own destiny. And at that point I didn't hate poverty anymore, because I knew it was only temporary. I knew I could change that. It was incredibly liberating for me, made all the difference.

To continue on that theme of education, in 1831 Alexis de Tocqueville came to America to study this country. The Europeans were fascinated. How could a fledgling nation, barely 50 years old already be competing with them on virtually every level? This was impossible. De Tocqueville was going to sort it out. He looked at our government and he was duly impressed by the three branches of government—four now because now we have special interest groups, but it was only three back in those days. He said, "WOW, this is really something," and then he said, "but let me look at their educational system," and he was blown away. You see, anybody who had finished the second grade was completely literate. He could find a mountain man on the outskirts of society who could read the newspaper and could have a political discussion . . . could tell him how the government worked.

If you really want to be impressed, take a look at the chapter on education in my latest book, *America the Beautiful*, which I wrote with my wife—it came out last year, and in that education chapter you will see questions extracted from

a sixth-grade exit exam from the 1800s—a test you had to
pass to get your sixth-grade certificate. I doubt most college
graduates today could pass that test. We have dumbed things
down to that level. And the reason that is so dangerous is
because the people who founded this nation said that our
system of government was designed for a well-informed and
educated populace. And when they become less informed,
they become vulnerable. Think about that . . . our system of
government. That is why education is so vitally important.

Now some people say, "Ahhh, you're overblowing it,
things aren't that bad, and you're a doctor, a neurosurgeon.
Why are you concerned about these things?" Got news for
you. FIVE doctors signed the Declaration of Independence.
Doctors were involved in the framing of the Constitution,
the Bill of Rights . . . a whole bunch of things. It's only been
in recent decades that we've extracted ourselves, which I
think is a big mistake.

We need doctors, we need scientists, engineers. We need
all those people involved in government, not just lawyers. I
don't have anything against lawyers, but you know, here's
the thing about lawyers . . . I'm sorry, but I got to be truthful . . . got to be truthful—what do lawyers learn in law
school? To win . . . by hook or by crook . . . you've got to win.
So you got all these Democrat lawyers, and you got all these
Republican lawyers and their sides want to win. We need to
get rid of that. What we need to start thinking about is, how
do we solve problems?

Now, before I get shot, let me finish. I don't like to bring
up problems without coming up with solutions. My wife and
I started the Carson Scholars Fund 16 years ago after we

heard about an international survey looking at the ability of eighth graders in 22 countries to solve math and science problems, and we came out number 21 out of 22. We only barely beat out number 22 . . . very concerning.

We'd go to these schools and we'd see all these trophies: All-State Basketball, All-State Wrestling, All-State this, that, and the other. The quarterback was the big man on campus. What about the intellectual superstar? What did they get? A National Honor Society pin? A pat on the head, "There, there little nerd?" Nobody cared about them. And is it any wonder that sometimes the smart kids try to hide? They don't want anybody to know that they are smart? This is not helping us as a nation. So we started giving out scholarships from all backgrounds for superior academic performance and demonstration of humanitarian qualities. Unless you cared about other people, it didn't matter how smart you were. We've got plenty of people like that. We don't need those. We need smart people who care about other people.

We would give them money. The money would go into a trust. They would get interest on it. When they would go to college they would get the money. But also the school gets a trophy, every bit as impressive as any sports trophy—and it goes right out there with the others. They get a medal. They get to go to a banquet. We try to put them on the same kind of pedestal as we do the all-state athletes. Now I have nothing against athletics or entertainment, please believe me. I'm from Baltimore. The Ravens won. This is great—okay. But— but what will maintain our position in the world? The ability to shoot a 25-foot jump shot or the ability to solve a quadratic equation? We need to put the things into proper perspective.

Many teachers have told us that when we put a Carson Scholar in their classroom, the GPA of the whole class goes up over the next year. It's been very gratifying. We started 16 years ago with 25 scholarships in Maryland, now we've given out more than 5,000 and we are in all 50 states. But we've also put in reading rooms. These are fascinating places that no little kid could possibly pass up. And uh, they get points for the amount of time they spend in there reading, and the number of books they read. They can trade the points for prizes. In the beginning they do it for the prizes, but it doesn't take long before their academic performance begins to improve.

And we particularly target Title I schools where the kids come from homes with no books and they go to schools with no libraries. Those are the ones who drop out. We need to truncate that process early on because we can't afford to waste any of those young people. You know, for every one of those people that we keep from going down that path, that path of self-destruction and mediocrity, that's one less person you have to protect yourself and your family from. One less person you have to pay for in the penal or the welfare system. One more taxpaying productive member of society who may invent a new energy source or come up with a cure for cancer. They are all important to us and we need every single one of them. It makes a difference. And when you go home tonight, read about it, Carson Scholars Fund, carson scholars.org.

But why is it so important that we educate our people? Because we don't want to go down the same pathway as many other pinnacle nations that have preceded us. I think particularly about ancient Rome. Very powerful. Nobody could even challenge them militarily. But what happened to them? They destroyed themselves from within . . . moral decay, fiscal irresponsibility . . . they destroyed themselves. If you don't think that can happen to America, you get out your books and you start reading.

But you know, we can fix it. Why can we fix it? Because we're smart. We have some of the most intellectually gifted people leading our nation. All we need to do is remember what our real responsibilities are so that we can solve the problems.

I think about these problems all the time. And you know, my role model was Jesus. And He used parables to help people understand things. And one of our big problems right now (and like I said, I'm not politically correct, so I'm sorry), but you know—our deficit is a big problem. Think about it. And our national debt—$16 and 1/2 trillion dollars—you think that's not a lot of money? I'll tell you what! Count one number per second, which you can't even do because once you get to a thousand it will take you longer than a second, but . . . one number per second. You know how long it would take you to count to 16 trillion? 507,000 years—more than a half a million years to get there. We have to deal with this.

Here's the parable: A family falls on hard times. Dad loses his job or is demoted . . . gets part-time work. He has 5 children. He comes to the 5 children, he says, "We're going to have to reduce your allowance." Well, they're not happy about it but . . . he says, ". . . except for John and Susan. They're . . . they're special. They get to keep their allowance.

In fact, we'll give them more." How do you think that's going to go down? Not too well. Same thing happens. Enough said.

What about our taxation system? So complex there is no one who can possibly comply with every jot and tittle of our tax system. If I wanted to get you, I could get you on a tax issue. That doesn't make any sense. What we need to do is come up with something that is simple.

And when I pick up my Bible, you know what I see? I see the fairest individual in the Universe: God. And He's given us a system. It's called tithe. Now we don't necessarily have to pay 10% but it's the principle. He didn't say, "If your crops fail, don't give me any tithes." He didn't say, "If you have a bumper crop, give me triple tithes." So there must be something inherently fair about proportionality. You make $10 billion dollars you put in a billion. You make $10 you put in $1. Of course, you've got to get rid of the loopholes. But now some people say, "Well that's not fair because it doesn't hurt the guy who made $10 billion dollars as much as the guy who made $10." Where does it say you have to hurt the guy? He's just put a billion dollars in the pot. We don't need to hurt him.

It's that kind of thinking . . . it's that kind of thinking that has resulted in 602 banks in the Cayman Islands. That money needs to be back here, building our infrastructure and creating jobs. And we're smart enough . . . we're smart enough to figure out how to do that.

We've already started down the path to solving one of the other big problems: health care. We need to have good health care for everybody. It's the most important thing that a person can have. Money means nothing, titles mean nothing when you don't have your health. But we've got to figure out efficient ways to do it. We spend a lot of money on health care, twice as much per capita as anybody else in the world, and yet not very efficient. What can we do?

Here's my solution. When a person is born, give him a birth certificate, an electronic medical record, and a health savings account [HSA], to which money can be contributed, pretax from the time you are born, to the time you die. When you die, you can pass it on to your family members so that when you're 85 years old and you've got 6 diseases, you're not trying to spend up everything. You're happy to pass it on and there's nobody talking about death panels. That's number one.

Also, for the people who are indigent, who don't have any money, we can make contributions to their HSA each month because we already have this huge pot of money. Instead of sending it to some bureaucracy, let's put it into HSAs. Now they have some control over their own health care and what do you think they're going to do? They're going to learn very quickly how to be responsible. When Mr. Jones gets that diabetic foot ulcer, he's not going to the emergency room and blowing a big chunk of it. He's going to go to the clinic. He learns that very quickly . . . gets the same treatment. In the emergency room they send him out. In the clinic they say, now let's get your diabetes under control so that you're not back here in three weeks with another problem. That's how we begin to solve these kinds of problems. It's much more complex than that, and I don't have time to go into it all, but we CAN do all of these things because we are smart people.

And let me begin to close here by another parable: Sea

Captain. And he's out on the sea near the area where the *Titanic* went down. And they look ahead and there's a bright light right there . . . another ship, he figures. He tells his signaler, "Signal that ship: Deviate 10 degrees to the south." Back comes the message, "No, you deviate 10 degrees to the north." Well, he's a little bit incensed, you know. He says, "Send a message, 'This is CAPTAIN Johnson. Deviate 10 degrees to the south.'" Back comes the message, "This is Ensign 4th Class Reilly. Deviate 10 degrees to the north." Now Captain Johnson is really upset. He says, "Send him a message, 'This is a naval destroyer.'" Back comes the message, "This is a lighthouse." Enough said.

Now, what about the symbol of our nation? The eagle. The bald eagle. It's an interesting story how we chose that, but a lot of people think we call it the bald eagle because it looks like it has a bald head. That's not the reason. It comes from the Old English word *piebald*, which means crowned with white. And we just shortened it to *bald*. Now, use that the next time you see somebody who thinks they know everything. You'll get 'em on that one.

But, why is that eagle able to fly . . . high . . . forward? Because it has two wings: a left wing and a right wing. Enough said.

And I want to close with this story: Two hundred years ago this nation was involved in a war, the War of 1812. The British, who are now our good friends, thought that we were young whippersnappers. It was time for us to become a colony again. They were winning that war . . . marching up the eastern seaboard, destroying city after city. Destroyed Washington, DC, burned down the White House. Next stop . . .

Baltimore. As they came into the Chesapeake Bay, that armada of ships . . . war ships as far as the eye could see. It was
looking grim. Fort McHenry standing right there. General
Armistead, who was in charge of Fort McHenry, had a large
American flag commissioned to fly in front of the fort. The
admiral in charge of the British fleet was offended, and said
"Take that flag down. You have until dusk to take that flag
down. If you don't take it down, we will reduce you to ashes."

There was a young amateur poet on board by the name
of Francis Scott Key, sent by President Madison to try to obtain the release of an American physician who was being
held captive. He overheard the British plans. They were not
going to let him off the ship. He mourned. As dusk approached he mourned for his fledgling young nation, and as
the sun fell, the bombardment started. Bombs bursting in
air . . . missiles . . . so much debris. He strained, trying to see,
was the flag still there? Couldn't see a thing. All night long it
continued. At the crack of dawn he ran out to the banister.
He looked, straining his eyes, but all he could see was dust
and debris.

And then there was a clearing and he beheld the most
beautiful sight he had ever seen . . . the torn and tattered
Stars and Stripes still waving. And many historians say that
was the turning point in the War of 1812. We went on to win
that war and to retain our freedom. And if you had gone
onto the grounds of Fort McHenry that day, you would have
seen at the base of that flag, the bodies . . . of soldiers who
took turns propping up that flag! They would not let that flag
go down because they believed in what that flag symbolized.
And what did it symbolize? One nation, under God, [ap-

plause] indivisible, with liberty and justice for all. Thank you. God Bless.

Many have commented that the president appeared to be uncomfortable during my speech, but I was not paying particular attention to him or his reactions, as my comments were really directed more at the American people than the people on the dais. At the conclusion of the program, the president approached me to shake my hand and thank me for my participation. He did not appear to be hostile or angry, but within a matter of minutes after the conclusion of the program, I received a call from some of the prayer breakfast organizers saying that the White House was upset and requesting that I call the president and apologize for offending him. I said that I did not think that he was offended and that I didn't think that such a call was warranted.

Although I thought the speech was good—the audience response was overwhelming, I had no idea that it would go viral and that literally millions of people would be talking about it over the next few days. This reaction was a reflection of the fact that the American people are excited to know that they are not the only ones who value common sense. People are also excited when they see one of their fellow citizens unintimidated by political correctness and unafraid to express his opinions.

The conservative news outlets were very excited about the talk and in fact the *Wall Street Journal* penned an article entitled, "Ben Carson for President." Requests for my appearance on television and radio exploded and there was and continues to be much speculation about my political future. Over the years, there have been many attempts to get me to throw my hat into the political arena. I have been offered support from around the country and tremendous financial resources if I decide to run for national office. But I have not felt called to run. I suspect that there are many others who think logically and are interested in a political future who might be better candidates than myself. Nevertheless, if I felt called by God to officially enter the world of politics, I certainly would not hesitate to do so.

However, at the moment, I believe the more important thing that can be done with the platform I have been given is to try to convince the American populace that we are not one another's enemies even if a (D) is by some of our names and an (R) by the names of others. Knowing that the future of my grandchildren and everyone else's is put in jeopardy by a continuation of reckless spending, godless government, and mean-spirited attempts to silence critics leaves me with little choice but to continue to expound on the principles outlined in my prayer breakfast speech and to fight for a bright future for America.

ONE NATION

SAVING OUR FUTURE

Godliness exalts a nation, but sin is a disgrace to any people.

PROVERBS 14:34

Several years ago I took a trip to Alaska, and my hosts offered to send me on an excursion in their private plane to see the glaciers in the area. I was extremely excited and eagerly accepted the offer. I was less excited when I saw the single-engine prop plane that would be used by the pilot. He assured me that he had flown this mission many times and that the plane was very safe, so we headed out.

As the plane took off, I marveled at the beautiful scenery. As we flew over the mountaintop and dropped into the valley, it almost seemed as if we were on another planet. The glaciers were awe inspiring and I quietly thanked God for the opportunity to view these natural wonders.

As I was enjoying the sights, heavy cloud cover descended on the valley severely obscuring our view. The small plane was not equipped for instrument-only flight, so the pilot announced that we were going to climb through the clouds as rapidly as we could without going into a stall, and that we should clear the mountaintops that surrounded us. He spoke calmly, but I could detect the uncertainty in his voice. Deeply concerned, I entered into prayer and reminded myself that God is in charge even when we are in grave danger.

After several intense minutes of upward flight, there was a break in the clouds and we cleared the mountain peaks by just a few feet. Relieved, I thanked the pilot for his quick and decisive action that saved our lives. I was never so happy to be on the ground as when we landed at the small airstrip.

Our nation is in trouble today, and our only chance is to take quick and decisive action the way the pilot did in Alaska. Shrugging and hoping that something good would happen was not a viable choice for us as our plane hurtled toward the mountain, and it is not a wise choice for us today. Doing everything we could while beseeching the mercies of God paid big dividends in the Alaskan sky, and prayerful action could make all the difference in the problems America faces now.

Many Americans argue that our nation's future does not need to be saved and that we are in very good shape. They think that only partisans are skeptical about our future and that people say negative things in order to make the current administration look bad. They see the beautiful view that is America, but they don't have the common sense and wisdom to look for the lowering clouds that obscure the mountains.

It is true that we are enjoying the benefits of the system set up by our founders, and we are relatively quite comfortable because previous generations have made good choices. Nevertheless, the fog has been gathering for years, and we must act quickly and decisively to deal with substantial issues if we don't want to destroy our children's future.

A quick glance at a newspaper should be enough to perceive the warning signs. As far as education is concerned, we have made a lot of progress in being politically correct, but very little progress in basic education, particularly in areas like math and science. The secular progressive movement completely denies any moral backsliding and feels that we have made substantial progress as a nation with respect to great moral issues like abortion, gay marriage, and helping the poor, but in reality we are losing our moral compass and are caught up in elitism and bigotry. On top of that, our national debt and the passage of Obamacare are threatening the financial future of our nation. Worst of all, we seem to have lost our ability to discuss important issues respectfully and courteously and cannot come together enough to begin to solve our problems.

We each need to take an active role in changing the course of our nation if we are to live up to the motto "one nation under God, indivisible, with liberty and justice for all." We are the pinnacle nation in the world right now, but if the examples of Egypt, Greece, Rome, and Great Britain teach us anything, it is that pinnacle nations are not guaranteed their place forever. If we fail to rediscover the basic principles of common sense, manners, and morality, we will go the same way they did. Fortunately, our downward pathway is not an inexorable one. It is not too late to learn from the mistakes of those who preceded us and take the kinds of corrective action that will ensure a promising future for those who come after us.

Communities, political parties, business organizations, the

news media, educational institutions, and the government can all work to turn our nation around, but the most important changes will be made by you and me, the American individuals. Each of us can control only our own behavior, but if we all take action individually, our actions will collectively have a significant impact on the direction of our nation. As individuals, we can educate ourselves and our children, cultivate the art of compromise, pray for wisdom, and hold our representatives accountable. Each of us can positively affect our nation just by making ourselves (and those in our spheres of influence) aware of the fact that we are being used as pawns by those who try to tell us what we should think as opposed to using our own common sense.

As an example of cloudy thinking that threatens common sense, consider the recent furor over voter ID cards. I travel to many nations of the world, and recently I've taken it upon myself to ask citizens of those other countries how they prevent voter fraud. I have yet to find a nation that does not require some type of official voter identification card or mechanism to ensure that the voter is who they say they are. This is basic common sense, yet some members of our society who have co-opted the media have convinced ordinary Americans that there is some type of discrimination going on when we require the same thing of those voting in our country. This would not even be an issue if political groups weren't trying to curry favor with certain groups of voters. Instead of being whipped into a frenzy over a nonissue, it is my hope and prayer that individual Americans will educate themselves on this issue, seek to understand one another's values, allow common sense to prevail, and reject those who try to politicize almost everything to their own advantage.

When I was a child, there was a common saying: "Sticks and stones may break my bones but names will never hurt me." I'm not sure that children today have ever heard that expression and certainly the adults don't seem to know it any longer. Special interest groups tell our country's citizens that they should be easily offended by simple words or suggestions. By taking umbrage so readily, people shift the discussion from the subject matter to the person making the comment, which is a desirable thing to do only if you don't have a good argument. This is also a good way to keep people at one another's throats constantly so they can't form a united front and deal logically with the many real issues facing the nation. Individually, Americans need to choose to be the bigger person, overlook offense, and be willing to have candid discussions about volatile issues.

There have been many stories recently about the bullying epidemic that seems to be occurring in our public school system. We should not be terribly surprised by this because children emulate what they see adults doing. One does not have to look at television for very long or listen to the radio for an extended period before one sees supposedly rational and mature adults vehemently attacking one another, calling each other names and acting like third graders. I have grown used to dealing with people who resort to name-calling at the drop of a hat by saying, "Now that you have had an opportunity to engage in a gratuitous attack, is it possible for us to return to the subject matter at hand?" I refuse to engage in the grade-schoolyard tactics of name-calling and mean-spirited comments when we have so many important issues to solve. We can help our nation quite a bit if we refrain from getting into our respective corners and throwing hand grenades at each other, and instead try to understand the other's viewpoint, reject the stifling of political correctness, and engage in intelligent civil discussion.

A suitably thick skin, common sense, and manners are of limited use without education. I'm always fascinated by some of the "man on the street" episodes on *The Tonight Show with Jay Leno* or *Watters' World* on Fox, where Jay or Jesse asks people for very basic information regarding the significance of a particular day or some historical event and many of them have no clue about the right answer. Our nation's founders felt very strongly that our system of government could only survive with a well-informed and educated populace. They understood that if the populace reached the point of not being able to critically analyze information, it would easily fall prey to slick politicians and unethical news media. All citizens need to arm themselves with a basic knowledge of American history and stay abreast of current events, analyzing them with respect to history. Knowledge is power and at a time when the people are becoming increasingly impotent while the government grows larger and more powerful, it is vital that we arm ourselves with knowledge.

Finally, each of us must have courage. I have encountered countless thousands of Americans, as I've traveled around the country recently giving speeches, who resonate very strongly with the concepts that I'm putting forward but who have been beaten down. They have mistaken the false unity of political correctness and submission for the true unity that comes with liberty, justice, and responsibility. This unity doesn't succeed without some conflict, but it is far healthier than silence and is worth the fight. I've been spreading the word that we must have enough backbone to stand up to the secular progressives who insist on fundamentally changing America into something that we would not recognize as our hard-won government of, by, and for the people. Because there are consequences for standing up for your beliefs in the current distorted version of America, one has to be very courageous when standing up to malicious influences or even while engaging in healthy dialogue with our neighbors about important issues.

The bottom line is that our country is in the process of undergoing fundamental radical changes while rapidly moving away from the "can-do" attitude that made us the most prosperous and beneficent superpower the world has ever known. If each of us sits back and expects someone to take action, it will soon be too late. But as of today, it is still not too late to join the battle to save our nation and pass on to our children and grandchildren something we can all be proud of.

PART ONE

—

CAUSES OF DISUNITY
AND DECLINE

2

POLITICAL CORRECTNESS

Those who love to talk will experience the consequences, for
the tongue can kill or nourish life.

PROVERBS 18:21

When I was a teenager, my neighbor had a dog that appeared to
be quite vicious. If anyone walked near that home, the dog
would come running toward the fence, barking and snarling,
sending the passerby rapidly along his way. His ferociousness
actually changed the behavior of people in the neighborhood,
who began to avoid walking down the alley when the dog was
outside.

Feeling that the dog should not be ruining the neighborhood, I began reading books about dogs and their behavior to
see what I could do. I discovered that dogs tend to react to the
reaction of the human or other animal it is trying to frighten—
if the person they bark at shows fear, the dog decides its antics
are effective. If the person shows no fear, the dog will give up.

It took a lot of courage, but I decided to repeatedly walk by
the fence and completely ignore the dog. It took about a month
before the dog realized that I would not react, but eventually he

stopped trying to frighten me and would simply lie down quietly as I walked by.

Today's political correctness operates in the same way as that dog. Self-appointed political correctness police (PCP) have set up speech guidelines that go far beyond the requirements of kindness, good manners, education, and tact. They forbid the use of the word *slavery* by conservatives, the mention of Nazism by conservatives, or the mention of homosexuality in anything other than a positive context, to name a few of their rules. Going even further, they continually grow their list of terms they believe are offensive, tripping up innocent people with their increasingly strict speech code. By bludgeoning people who violate these rules, the PCP establish a chilling control over the speech of a nation that was founded on the principles of freedom of speech. Intent on managing the national conversation, they mock and belittle anyone who violates their tenets of speech or behavior with such ferocity that few people will dare trespass their boundaries. For example, a few years ago, Lawrence Summers, then president of Harvard, mentioned that men and women might be wired differently. His comments drew a fierce attack from the PCP that may well have influenced his decision to resign his position.

I had my own run-in with the PCP when I said that I thought Obamacare was the worst thing in our country since slavery. My point was that we the American people were turning over to the government control of our most precious resource—our health. The implications of such a shift of power (where we have no choice but to purchase the only prescribed product—Obamacare), are profound in a society that is supposed to be free and centered around freedom of choice. Once we give the government this kind of power, it is naïve to believe that it will stop here in its quest for total control of our lives. The PCP wanted to immediately divert the argument away from this fundamental truth, so they said I thought Obamacare was an evil equal to slavery, when I was merely pointing out that this particular attempt at health care reform takes us the first step away from liberty.

Many well-meaning Americans have bought into the PC speech code, thinking that by being extra careful not to offend anyone we will achieve unity. What they fail to realize is that this is a false unity that prevents us from talking about important issues and is a Far Left strategy to paralyze us while they change our nation. People have been led to become so sensitive that fault can be found in almost anything anyone says because somewhere, somehow, someone will be offended by it.

To stop this, Americans need to recognize what is happening, speak up courageously, avoid fearful or angry responses, and ignore the barking and snarling as we put political correctness to bed forever. This is the reason why I choose to continue speaking out despite the many efforts of the secular progressives to discredit and silence me. It is also the reason why I continue to encourage Americans to stand up for the freedoms that were hard-won and must be preserved if we are to remain a free society.

Political Correctness Stifles Dialogue

Open discussions of political and social issues are key to healthy unity. Society works very much like a marriage in the sense that open communication facilitates harmony. In almost all marriages that end in divorce, there is a serious breakdown in communication, followed by false assumptions and outright warfare. One of the first things a marriage counselor does is get the warring parties to sit down and open up to each other. Two people may perceive the same event very differently, and gaining an understanding of the other person's perspective can be the first step to healing a broken marriage. If fear or anger prevents either person from expressing his or her perspective, there is no hope for the relationship.

In our country today, we act much like those warring spouses who want nothing more than to get rid of each other. Political correctness has thrown a veil of silence over our important discussions. Rather than asking those with whom we disagree to clearly state their case, we set up rules of political correctness that mandate that their perspective must be the same as ours. We then demonize those with whom we disagree and as a result fail to reach any consensus that might solve our problems.

The only people who can resolve this problem are "we the people." We do not have to yield to pop culture, Hollywood, politicians, and the media who are the primary enforcers of political correctness. We need to simply ignore the "barking" and act like mature adults who can tolerate hearing something about which we disagree and still remain civil and open-minded.

Who Benefits from Hypersensitivity?

While most people buying into the PC code are well meaning and just want to get along with everyone, the ones who bark and snarl the most are those on the Far Left who cultivate political correctness in order to forward their own agendas. In his famous book, *Rules for Radicals*, Saul Alinsky, an activist and organizer of the Far Left, makes it clear that leftists trying to effect change are to have no conversations with their opponents, because open discussion could lend credence to their opponents' arguments and humanize them in the sight of the public. He argued that activists must demonize their opponents and get the larger society to recognize the activists as the ones who will deliver society from the demons. As Alinsky suggests, cultivating hypersensitivity to perceived slights by conservatives is a convenient way to halt important conversations and to demonize opponents.

Unfortunately, hypersensitivity is not limited to those on the Left. Conservative politicians have also adopted the strategy of feigned offense. The Right tends to be hypersensitive about blaming Bush for economic problems and the double standard of the media. Even though these problems are real, hypersensitive conservatives sometimes see bias where it doesn't exist, defend Bush when they don't need to, or even shut down a discussion because of a perceived slight.

While we all have a tendency to say "See, they did it too!" in order to justify wrongdoing, we must start focusing on what is right or wrong and not on what someone else did. It is imperative that each of us, whatever side we are on, begins to act like adults who can find real solutions instead of pointing the finger at others or running away crying because someone disagreed with us.

It's Not All About You

When talking about hypersensitivity in our society, it is important to distinguish between those who are truly sensitive to comments and those instigators and manipulators with feigned sensitivity and outrage. To the first group I would say it's time to grow up and start thinking about what you can do to contribute to society's well-being instead of choosing to be a victim of speech that is sometimes intentionally cruel and at other times completely innocent. The best way not to be easily injured by others' speech is to step out of the center of the circle so everything is not about you. By thinking about others and looking at things from other people's perspectives, there is much less time to feel that someone is picking on you or your interests.

In a previous book, I mentioned that when I was an intern at Johns Hopkins back in 1977, the sight of a black physician was decidedly rare. Often when I would go onto a hospital ward while wearing my surgical scrubs, a nurse would say, "I'm sorry, but Mr. Patient is not quite ready to be taken to the operating room yet," assuming that I was an orderly. After many years of hard work to achieve the title of doctor, many might say that I would have been justified in reacting angrily to the suggestion that I was an orderly, especially given the racial overtones of the misunderstanding. However, I tried to look at things from the nurse's perspective. The only black males she had seen come onto that ward wearing surgical scrubs were orderlies who were coming to pick up or deliver a patient. Why would she think differently in my case? A highly sensitive individual would have created a scene and everyone would have felt uncomfortable. I would simply say in those situations, "I'm sorry that Mr. Patient isn't ready yet, but I'm Dr. Carson and I'm here for another reason."

The offending nurse would often be so embarrassed that I actually felt sorry for her or him and would say, "It's quite all right and you don't need to feel bad." I would be very nice to that person, and I would have another friend for life. That was a whole lot better than having someone who would always feel ashamed, embarrassed, or hostile when they saw me.

Some might say that by allowing ignorant slights or insults to go, I capitulated to the racism of the day, but that's not the case. Instead, by realizing that the nurse's statement really wasn't a reflection of careful judgment about me, I was able to remain calm and gently correct the offender. I guarantee you that both the nurse's mistake and my response reduced the lingering effects of racism in her mind just as well, if not better, than an angry outburst on my part would have.

Political correctness aside, people do say ignorant, insensitive, and even malicious things. However, most of our public fights over racism, sexism, and every other "ism" could be easily resolved if the injured party expected the best of the offender and corrected the offensive statement in a kind and rational manner. We all have choices in the way we react to the words we hear. Our lives and the lives of all those around us will be significantly improved if we choose to react positively rather than negatively.

Faux Hypersensitivity

To the second group of hypersensitives, those who are feigning hurt to make a point, I would say you need to decide where your priorities are. Are you interested in the unity and our nation's well-being or is it more important for you to further a political agenda that is not consistent with the founding principles of unity in this country? Political correctness and hypersensitivity block discussion of important social issues while they are being changed—exactly the time when it is most important to discuss them.

An excellent example of how these people work occurred about a month after the National Prayer Breakfast when on national television I was asked about my opinion regarding gay marriage. I immediately stated that I believe marriage is between a man and a woman and that no group has the right to change the definition of marriage to suit their needs. By way of example of groups that engaged in nontraditional sexual relationships, I mentioned NAMBLA (North American Man/Boy Love Association) and people who engage in bestiality. My point was to emphasize that marriage is a long-standing tradition and there is no necessity to change the definition now, regardless of which group wants to change it.

The secular progressives seized upon the opportunity to distort the meaning of what I said and deviate the conversation away from the definition of marriage by instead focusing on me and trying to paint me as a homophobe who thinks that gay marriage is equivalent to bestiality. Nothing could be further from the truth. I appeared both on CNN and MSNBC to explain that I didn't think that there was equivalency between the groups mentioned in my answer and to state unequivocally that I had no intention of offending anyone, but I still believe in traditional marriage. The objective media found that explanation satisfactory, but the secular progressive media continued to state that I think that gay marriage and bestiality are the same. This is a very instructive example of how they distort words and meanings, and then cling to the created lies in an attempt to destroy enemies.

Around the same time, a group of gay activists at the Johns

Hopkins School of Medicine began their mission as instigators, accusing me of being a homophobe. I was scheduled to be the commencement speaker at the Johns Hopkins School of Medicine as well as at the Johns Hopkins School of Education, but decided to withdraw because of the controversy the instigators had successfully created. After years of hard work by the students, I did not want their graduation ceremony to be about me rather than about them and their achievements.

I received several messages from students who were very disappointed that I would not be speaking at their commencement. Some even threatened to protest if I did not speak. The thing that saddened me most was the fact that many of them indicated that they were afraid to speak out because of potential repercussions from the administration. I certainly like to think that these fears were unfounded, but the fact that they exist at all is troubling. Like so many thousands of Americans I have encountered across the nation, these students had been beaten into submission by secular progressives who have no regard for such fundamental American principles as freedom of speech when that speech is not in agreement with their philosophies. Political correctness has effectively removed their point of view, as well as their rights, from the debate.

Prior to my decision to withdraw as commencement speaker, I spoke to some prominent members of the gay community at Johns Hopkins. In doing so I found out two important things: First, bestiality is particularly abhorrent in the gay community and the mention of it evokes a very emotional response. Had I known that, I would have avoided the topic, since the last thing I wanted to do was to cause unnecessary offense and distract from the matters at hand.

Second, I asked if there was any position a person could take that did not include approval of gay marriage that would be acceptable to the gay community. After some consideration, I was told that there really was no other acceptable position. This explains why there was such a ferocious attack on my comments—there really was no argument that could have been made that would not have drawn an emotional response instead of a rational argument.

Responding to the PC Police

Not only is it important for Americans to communicate about difficult issues, but the method and tone of communication are also very important. Abrasive and reactionary speech can be at least as bad as silence, feeding right into the hands of the PCP. Saul Alinsky advised his followers to level sharp attacks against their opponents with the goal of goading them into rash counterattacks that would then discredit them. To avoid falling into this trap, those of us who are interested in civil discussion should prepare ourselves to refrain from reacting in fear or anger to those who disagree with us or even attack us.

I frequently remind my attackers that our greater purpose is to engage in intelligent conversation and solve problems. Most who disagree with me are good, intelligent people who also want to solve problems in a reasonable manner. As for those who are not so well intentioned, it is very difficult for them to continue attacking someone who is calm and reasonable. They usually realize fairly quickly that they are the ones who look like fools if they refuse to engage in problem solving.

It is particularly important when dealing with adversaries to know what points you want to make while remaining focused. This makes constant interruptions, attacks, and attempts to change the subject more difficult. If you are an effective representative of American values, the secular progressives will make every attempt to destroy your character by exposing any mistakes, misstatements, or misdeeds from your past. Naturally, there are no perfect people, present company included, which makes the threats of exposure extremely potent. If a misdeed from your past is exploited, it is best to admit to it, condemn it, and ask, "What more do you want?"

Sometimes I am asked, "How do you maintain your cool when faced with ridiculous claims and statements by your opponents?" There was a time when I was a hothead, and my temper wreaked havoc in my life until I learned to take myself out of the center of the circle. The real key to staying cool and calm is to relinquish selfishness and always consider the feelings of others. When someone is being particularly mean and nasty, I simply think to myself, *He or she used to be a cute little baby, I wonder what happened?* Thinking about that question will soften your attitude and lessen the likelihood of an inflammatory confrontation.

As we discussed earlier in this book, offense and sensitivity are frequently feigned for the purpose of garnering sympathy and further reinforcing the validity of political correctness. However, two can play that game. When the offended party proclaims the injury you have wrought upon them with your words, say something to the effect of: "I can see that you were deeply hurt by my choice of words. It was not my intention to hurt you and for that I am sorry. Now I would like for you to know what I intended to communicate to you and I will use different words that will hopefully convey the spirit of my thoughts and allow our discussion to continue." If the offended party was truly offended, that will be a sufficient statement, but if they were only pretending to be offended, they will continue to harp on their perceived mistreatment. This exercise is useful because it helps you learn what you are dealing with. If it is just a misunderstanding, frequently the conflict can be alleviated by this kind of open communication.

True Wounds

Sometimes a true wound can be so deep that it clouds the thoughts of the injured party to the point that they can no longer be objective. In such cases, continued explanations tend to result in diminishing returns or even exacerbations of the misunderstanding. I vividly remember the case of a disabled woman whom I greatly admire because she adopted many children with disabilities that were even greater than hers. Many of her children had complex neurosurgical problems that engaged my skills for many hours at a time. After caring for her many children over the years, one of them experienced a shunt malfunction that caused rapid accumulation of pressure in the head due to the spinal fluid's inability to escape. I rushed into the hospital in the middle of the night, even being stopped by the police for speeding. We operated on the child and repaired the shunt, but unfortunately the child suffered some brain damage and was never quite the same again. Despite explanations and a long-term relationship, I never saw that mother or any of her children again. I believe the emotional trauma was understandably more than she could handle. Sometimes you just have to realize that you cannot heal all wounds no matter how hard you try.

In today's political scene, some people are so traumatized by perceived past injustices that they cannot conceive of any good thing that a group member who they believe has been unfair to them can do. They tend to demonize these individuals for past wrongs perpetrated by others and there is no changing their minds. It is important for the demonized group to understand this mentality and patiently attempt to undo the damage that has resulted in such attitudes. Both Republicans and Democrats can benefit from this advice.

Our Heritage of Free Speech

Whether by creating hypersensitivity or drawing angry reactions, Alinsky's organizers' goal is to make the societal majority feel that their opinion is the minority opinion and that the organizers' opinion is the majority opinion. The ability to co-opt the mainstream media in this endeavor is a gigantic coup. If the majority of people who are rational, reasonable, and full of common sense feel that their opinions are out of sync with everyone else, it is easy to shut them up and beat them into submission. This is what has occurred in America today. Hopefully by bringing this to light, more people will see the necessity of seizing the banner of bravery just like Nathan Hale, Patrick Henry, and many others in the past who stood up to tyranny.

Why was freedom of speech so important to our nation's founders? Many had come from countries like England where verbally opposing the king frequently resulted in a jail sentence or even death. The founders also felt that the free exchange of ideas would result in better government and would prevent government from becoming too big and self-important. These are the very reasons we must once again insist on freedom of speech and expression, and we should be repulsed by the very idea of political correctness that muzzles the populace. Our government does not directly jail dissenters, but it can do so indirectly by expecting the IRS to harass those who oppose its policies. This should be something that completely outrages every American who understands the hard-fought freedoms of our nation, but many have been lulled to sleep by the gradual increase of political correctness and have yet to notice that our fundamental freedoms are in jeopardy.

It is tempting to simply acknowledge the corrosive effects of political correctness on freedom of speech and say that we will deal with this at some point in the future. The problem with that line of thinking is that the future may not arrive before catastrophic events intervene.

If we are to survive as a united nation, we must learn how to engage in civil discussion of our differences without becoming bitter enemies. We cannot fall for the Saul Alinsky trick of not having a conversation while trying to demonize each other. Let's talk about the tough issues without scrutinizing every word and castigating anyone who dares to violate the PC rules. There is nothing wrong with disagreement—in fact, if two people agree about everything, one of them isn't necessary. I believe we are all necessary so let's toss out the hypersensitivity and roll up our sleeves and start working together to solve our problems. If each of us is willing to extend the benefit of the doubt or overlook verbal missteps, political correctness will become impotent.

Action Steps

1. Try to identify one instance of artificial outrage. Explain to one other person why this is a contrived issue and outline the way it agitates people and cultivates political support for the agitators.
2. Readily apologize to a person who is offended by something you said. Explain what you had hoped to convey.
3. Attempt to politely disagree with someone who makes a political statement with which you disagree. (Be sure that you choose an appropriate setting.) Engage in a civil discussion of the matter.
4. Read Saul Alinsky's *Rules for Radicals* to get an idea of how the political correctness police work.

ELITISM

Pride goes before destruction, and haughtiness before a fall.

Coming from inner-city Detroit and going to Yale University represented an astronomical change in my surroundings and life. One of my freshman roommates had a twin brother matriculating at Princeton and a father who was a prominent physician. The other roommate was from a business family. They all seemed very rich to me, being the son of a divorced mother with less education than the maids who cleaned their houses. But my roommates' wealth and status was minor compared with some of the really rich kids on campus. Many were from very well-known families and traveled around with an entourage of sycophants and admirers. It was not unusual to see parents visiting campus in Rolls-Royces and limousines when I was a freshman and a sophomore. I was surrounded by elites.

But the way the elites presented themselves was changing. By the end of my sophomore year, the campus was already starting to become radicalized. The Black Panthers were idolized, and the most admired people on campus dressed like hippies and flower children. Marijuana and acid rock had become fashionable, and outward shows of affluence were frowned upon. Elitism on campus, which had previously been defined by wealth, was now defined by identification with the downtrodden people in society and a determination to use one's superior education and compassion to help them. As this generation of elites grew up, they began to occupy positions of importance in society, becoming college professors and administrators, national television producers, business managers, and politicians. Even though many still enjoyed the fruits of economic prosperity, they continued to identify with those people they considered to be oppressed by the system.

The makeup of today's elite class is psychologically and sociologically more complex than what I have just presented, but its development in the Ivy Leagues of the 1960s can explain the dichotomy between what the wealthy members of this class say and what they do. For the most part, they are incapable of seeing any hypocrisy in their own lives while examining with a microscope every facet of their perceived opponents' lives. They are very happy to give away other people's money, but guard their own purse strings possessively. The sad thing is that they have become so wise in their own eyes that they have lost objectivity, thus frequently rendering themselves quite useless when it comes to truly improving the lot of the downtrodden in our society.

Do the Elite Really Know Better Than the Rest of Us?

This arrogance is the chief characteristic of the elites I am concerned about. Wealth, education, and influence are all well and good, but when they lull those who hold them into a state of self-satisfaction where they are convinced of their own perfect wisdom and virtue and shield them from life's realities, we have a problem. Today's elites constantly talk about hubris in their opponents but seem unaware of their own lack of humility. They are thoroughly convinced that they are intellectually superior to those people who believe in God, creation, and the Bible, and many use positions of authority at colleges and universities to strictly enforce "open-mindedness" by pillorying any student or colleague who dares question their ideological rantings. The elite class also exists in the mainstream media where elite journalists try to be objective but simply cannot escape the influence of so many years of social propaganda. I believe that in their heart of hearts elites see themselves as society's savior, but they are blinded by pride to the results of their actions.

Not all elites are blinded by what they are doing. Very recently I was speaking to a major producer of a major left-wing television network who admitted that the electronic media today is a major propaganda tool used to manipulate society. We have never had this kind of access to the minds of the people and no one really knows the extent to which public opinion can be controlled. Most frightening, these secular progressive elites, as well as some right-leaning elites in the media, are willing to push the limits in order to see just how effective they can be with the imposition of their will upon the people.

Not all media personalities fit this characterization. Perhaps the greatest television journalist of all time, Walter Cronkite, was decidedly left wing in his political outlook, but was so professional in his reporting that most people were unaware of this. Unless the other elites can ever see the possibility of a flaw in their belief systems or are willing to be objective in their reporting, they are largely unreachable and have little intersection with common sense.

Politically, elitism knows no single party. Establishing policies that create dependency, like easy food stamps and subsidized health care for families making in excess of $80,000 per year, seems to stroke the egos of both Republican and Democrat elites who believe they are God's gift to mankind. However, if they examine the long-term consequences of what they are doing, some may begin to understand that true compassion warrants the investment of intellectual capital into finding ways that people can be elevated and imbued with the can-do attitude.

The Elite Oppression of Minority Communities

In order for elitism to flourish, there has to be another class of people who are willing to acknowledge the superiority of the chosen ones. Elites cultivate this obeisance by providing goodies to the less fortunate ones. In our society today, those goodies consist of multiple kinds of entitlement programs. As the dependency on these programs grows, the position of the elite class is solidified because they will always be seen as the providers who need to be protected from any threats of power redistribution. The elitists constantly find ways to proclaim their goodness and their necessity for the well-being of the "oppressed," while at the same time declaring how evil their opponents are, and how those evil people would utterly destroy any hope of a reasonable life for the oppressed if they were to gain power.

The truth is, the liberal policies of the elite class have done little to improve the lot of those who depend so much on them. In America's black communities, where the goodies have been flowing for decades, rather than seeing improvements in terms of upward mobility, we are seeing deteriorating family structure, increases in violent crimes, growing poverty, and growing dependence. Even with such a blatant record of failure, there is slavish devotion to the elite class who continue to promise more goodies in exchange for votes.

Black leaders like Booker T. Washington, George Washington Carver, and Dr. Martin Luther King, Jr., among others, were great proponents of self-reliance and self-help. I believe they would have been horrified to see the condition of the black community in America today despite their efforts to bring true economic liberation to this important group of Americans. Many of the elites from both parties embrace these men as heroes but propose social policies that do not encourage self-reliance; policies these men would never have approved. Based on their policies, I believe that they subconsciously think that some people are not capable of helping themselves.

Most of the elite are not humble enough to accept these kinds of criticisms and make changes. I guess that is why they are considered elite. Since we can't expect them to change, it's up to the rest of us to do all that we can to help those dependent on the elites to get on their feet. The elite class can't last long without the votes of these communities.

Escaping Subservience

One of the most important ways the African American community in particular can end its dependence on the elites is to lower the number of out-of wedlock births. As a result of the number of black babies born out of wedlock in recent years, there is a gigantic economic hole from which many in the community will have to climb out of to achieve the American Dream. That ascension needs to start immediately by teaching young women the importance of self-respect and the consequences of single motherhood—usually the end of the mother's educational endeavors, limiting her economic success and often condemning her child to poverty. (A 2013 article in *US News and World Report* by Steven Nelson titled "Census Bureau Links Poverty with Out-of-Wedlock Births" examines this phenomenon, which has been corroborated by many other journalistic sources.) At the same time, we need to provide affordable child care to enable single mothers to further their schooling and prepare for an increasingly technologically sophisticated world. We also have to demonstrate to these mothers that men are not going to disappear or be afraid of them after they obtain advanced education. This is a total myth and if anything, advanced education increases the opportunity to meet someone with similar accomplishments and goals. We must do everything we can to convince these young ladies that they are priceless and can make great contributions to all of mankind. When these valuable citizens gain appropriate self-esteem, they will avoid many careless mistakes and think more independently, weakening the hold the elites have on them.

Young black women aren't the only people needing to be

freed from the elites. A quarter of the young men in the black community are involved with the criminal justice system, which in many cases compromises their job prospects for the future. Worse than that is the fact that many end up being violently killed or taken off the streets by incarceration for long periods of time. In either case, tremendous intellectual talent is being wasted by a society that can ill afford such losses. Rather than imitating the elite and trying to make these young men feel like victims of discrimination or racism, we must look for ways to empower and help them realize their tremendous value to society.

Both the men and women in these communities need to be educated about basic economics and wealth creation. One of the reasons the Jewish, Korean, Vietnamese, and other communities have been able to thrive in the United States is that they have learned how to turn over the dollar in their own communities two or three times before sending it out into the larger community. By patronizing the constituents of their own neighborhoods, they allow local merchants and businesspeople to thrive, which not only provides jobs for others in the community but also gives them an opportunity to invest and grow their businesses. The more they grow, the more opportunities they are able to provide to those around them. I have a friend who started his own business as a young black man and has subsequently retired as a multimillionaire, and at least two other African American–owned businesses were started by others who got their initial breaks from him. Economic prosperity for one can mushroom into opportunities for many when greed and vice are not involved. Furthermore, this kind of thinking provides economic independence, and economic independence promotes ideological freedom, rather than creating voting blocs that can be taken for granted. If politicians have to compete for support, they will have to show results, which will be a big win for the black community.

Although understanding economic principles of wealth development is very important to oppressed communities and will go a long way toward liberating them from the influence of the elite class, even more important is education. When Frederick Douglass was a slave, the master's wife began teaching him to read after recognizing his exceptional intellectual gifts. When the master found out about this he was angry and instructed his wife to desist immediately, because he felt that education would light the fires of desire for freedom. He was absolutely right in this assessment, so Frederick Douglass went on to find other ways of educating himself. As a consequence, he was not only able to obtain his own freedom but played a vital role in the abolition of slavery as well as in the women's suffrage movement in the United States. He also lived in Europe and wielded significant influence there; many feel that his involvement and notoriety profoundly affected the decision of the British not to support the Confederacy during the Civil War.

During the fifties and sixties many people of all nationalities sacrificed life, limb, and physical freedom to win basic rights for blacks in America. Those rights included educational pursuits. During slavery, reconstruction, Jim Crow, and beyond, many blacks would have sacrificed almost anything for an opportunity to be educated. Sometimes, particularly when traveling north with their masters, slaves were able to witness how articulate and sometimes prosperous free, educated blacks were. They began to equate education with freedom. Even as a child growing up in Detroit and Boston, almost all of the adults in our neighborhood emphasized the importance of education and how it would allow me to go far beyond anything they had achieved. Today, even though those educational doors are no longer blocked, many of the people who sacrificed to open those doors would be disappointed to see the indifference with which many of the younger generation treat education.

It is time in America to empower the people through education, sound economic policies, and the return of honest and responsible media reporting. This will be no small undertaking, because the intellectually elite class will not relinquish their stranglehold without a fight. We must be encouraged by the fact that this is the United States of America: a place for, of, and by the people . . . and there is no place for elitism in our country.

Action Steps

1. Identify a member of an elite class and ask the person how he or she would recommend that you assist those stuck in poverty.
2. If you are a member of the elite class, ask yourself honestly what you have personally done in the last year to help lift someone from poverty.
3. Read and think about 2 Chronicles 7:14.
4. If you are offended by the previous suggestion, ask yourself why.

4

IGNORANCE AND FORGETFULNESS

Throw out the mocker, and fighting, quarrels, and insults will disappear. Anyone who loves a pure heart and gracious speech is the king's friend. The Lord preserves knowledge, but he ruins the plans of the deceitful.

PROVERBS 22:10-12

When I was a student at Southwestern High School in inner-city Detroit in the mid-to-late sixties, I was far from popular. By that time my lackluster academic performance during the early years had completely reversed and I was a quintessential nerd. I even carried a slide rule in a holster on my belt and belonged to the Chess Club. I grew quite accustomed to being ridiculed for not being "cool," but I was generally left alone because of my accomplishments in ROTC and because I was friends with some of the really tough guys, since I helped them with their school assignments.

When my wife and I attended my twenty-fifth Southwestern High School class reunion in 1994, I was astonished to see that so many of the really cool guys were now deceased, but I was even more amazed at the number of my former classmates who came up to me and said, "We are so proud of you and we tell our children and grandchildren about you all the time, and don't you remember how we used to encourage you when you were a student at Southwestern?" Of course I was polite, but I certainly didn't remember many encouraging words and in fact I vividly remember just the opposite.

It is natural to want to identify with success and distance oneself from failure and embarrassment and to avoid difficulty. This is why people undergo memory alterations as time passes and why we selectively forget painful knowledge. In medicine it is particularly important not to do this because people's lives could needlessly be put at risk by failure to accurately remember lessons of the past. I explicitly remember the case of an achondroplastic child (dwarfism) who I determined was in need of a highly specialized type of surgery to alleviate pressure on the brain stem. I wrote a letter and spoke to the gatekeeper at the insurance company to no avail. Because they wanted to save money, the insurance company determined that their in-network pediatric neurosurgeon could do the job. They were wrong and ended up paying twice, because I had to do corrective surgery. If they had heeded the medical knowledge that had summarized past lessons about this condition and its treatment, including the need for significant experience and a team approach, needless trauma and expense could have been avoided. Instead, they ignored key facts, willfully ignoring information that would have benefited a child's health and their bottom line.

Ignorance, whether it takes the form of revisionism or laziness, can hurt our nation too. If we don't know our true national history, we won't be able to recognize the way in which America is drifting. If we don't have enough basic information to manage our lives, we will give up our freedoms to those who promise to take care of us. It is time for us to stand up and educate ourselves and our children before we allow misinformation and ignorance to destroy our democratic republic.

Historical Revisionism

People frequently rewrite history to increase self-esteem and to clear their consciences of guilt for historical misdeeds. Historical revision can also go the other way, as historians attempt to discredit figures from the past. Early American history has been rewritten many times in both ways, to suit the beliefs of historians with different educational and philosophical agendas. For this reason, I rarely accept a single account of any historical event. Fortunately one can quickly get a sense of the truth by examining accounts from several different trusted sources.

There seems to be general consensus around the fact that the founders of this nation were men of great vision and intellect. They thoroughly studied the many civilizations that preceded us to try to determine the common pitfalls inherent in establishing a new government. With hard work, a lot of arguing, and finally an ecumenical prayer to God, they were able to put together a sixteen-and-one-third-page document known as the Constitution of the United States of America, one of the most admired governmental documents in history. This document encapsulated their vision of a nation where the freedom of the people to pursue their dreams was of paramount importance. It created a government that existed for the purpose of protecting the people from foreign invaders, protecting their assets and property, and facilitating their pursuit of happiness. The Constitution mandated minimal government interference in the everyday lives of the average citizen and arranged for the federal government to remain small, allowing state governments to be responsible for most of the legislation.

Our founders were deathly afraid that our government would do the same thing that virtually all other governments had done previously: expand continually, developing a voracious appetite for the resources of the people. They also feared that as the government expanded it would encroach upon the rights of the citizens. Finally, they were petrified that people would be complacent as the government expanded and would gradually relinquish their rights for a false sense of security. These great men wrote the Constitution the way they did to prevent the worst of their fears from coming true, creating a great and noble framework for virtuous government.

Some historical revisionists have denigrated the efforts of these great men and emphasized the fact that many of them were slaveholders or had some other flaw commonly seen in the culture at that time. The same historians also highlight our cruelty to the Japanese during World War II where we used hideous internment camps and detonated the only nuclear weapon against fellow human beings in history. They shine a bright light on the history of racism that was rampant throughout America, especially before the crusades of Dr. Martin Luther King Jr., and they repeatedly remind us of the atrocities witnessed during the Vietnam War, which we lost. By emphasizing these things and other wrongdoings, revisionists attempt to paint the United States as an opportunistic, uncaring, and savage nation in dire need of change.

There is no question that the United States, like every other nation, has made mistakes. However, what should be emphasized is that we are the first pinnacle nation of the world to wield such enormous power without brutally dominating other nations. We have helped rebuild nations ravaged by wars in which we took part and we have refused to confiscate oil, minerals, and other treasures found in nations we have helped or defeated. I believe it is fair to say that we are the most benign superpower the world has ever known. Furthermore, it is important that we maintain our pinnacle status, because if we lose it, we will be replaced by another world power that is unlikely to be nearly as benign.

In America, we have a proud history of accomplishment and of helping to save the world from tyranny. Our military is second to none and our technological achievements have transformed the world. We have moved from a nearly apartheid state to a multicultural society with enormous potential and strength that can be significantly enhanced by the kind of leadership that emphasizes a vision that unites everyone as opposed to exploiting differences to advance political causes.

If most of the people in the country believe that America is generally fair and decent, it becomes more difficult for Saul Alinsky types to recruit change agents and for those on the

Far Left to undermine our Constitution. Hence the constant bad-mouthing of our nation to impressionable young people, preparing them to be ripe for manipulation at the appropriate time. In the recent past, the Occupy Wall Street movement, which was replicated in many parts of the country, shows how easily physically destructive actions that compromise the rights and property of others can be incited in those who have been educated this way and also have an entitlement mentality.

Forgetting Our Christian Heritage

Some historical revisionists have also attempted to diminish the role of God and religion in our nation's past. A careful examination of the records, however, makes it quite clear that religion was a very important factor in the development of our nation. In 1831 when Alexis de Tocqueville came to America to try to unravel the secrets to the success of a fledgling nation that was already competing with the powers of Europe on virtually every level, he discovered that we had a fantastic public educational system that rendered anyone who had finished the second grade completely literate. He was more astonished to discover that the Bible was an important tool used to teach moral principles in our public schools. No particular religious denomination was revered, but rather commonly accepted biblical truths became the backbone of our social structure. Our founders did not believe that our society could thrive without this kind of moral social structure. In fact, it was our second president, John Adams, who said of our thoroughly researched and developed governing document, "Our Constitution was made only for a moral and religious people. It is wholly inadequate to the government of any other."

Adams's quote makes it clear that the founders did not want to extract God from our lives, but rather intended for his principles to be a central feature of our society. What they wanted to avoid was a theocracy-like state where the church dominated public policy or where the government dictated religious practice. That was the whole point of the separation clause of the First Amendment. The secular progressives have zoomed past the intent of the law and tried to replace it with their anti-God propaganda reinforced by bullying tactics. If Americans fail to educate themselves in American history, the revisionists will win this fight.

And right now it looks like they are winning. The secular progressive movement in America has been successful in removing all vestiges of faith in God from the public square. The very fact that people hesitate to say "Merry Christmas" to strangers lets you know just how successful they have been. Why are they so determined to remove God from our lives? They recognize that if we have no higher authority to answer to than man, we become gods unto ourselves and get to determine our own behavior. In their world, "If it feels good, do it." They can justify anything based on their ideology because in their opinion, there is no higher authority other than themselves to overrule them. They have a visceral reaction to the mention of God's word, because it tears at the fabric of their justification system.

Forgetting Dr. Martin Luther King Jr.'s Advice

The left wing secular progressives love to invoke the name of Dr. Martin Luther King Jr., but only in their historical revision would his views be compatible with theirs. The last thing he would have wanted to see was the culture of dependency that has developed among the very people he fought so hard to free. A strong opponent of godless ideology, Dr. King also rejected the idea that human beings are not responsible for their actions, arguing, "One of the most common tendencies of human nature is that of placing responsibility on some external agency for sins we have committed or mistakes we have made."

Later in the same speech, Dr. King spoke of several Americans who rose from less than optimal circumstances of heredity and environment to become successful and greatly admired individuals. Helen Keller, who was born blind and deaf, was able to overcome these hereditary traits to become one of the most admired people in the world! Franklin D. Roosevelt had infantile paralysis, but rose to become president of the United States. Marian Anderson was born in poverty in Philadelphia, but developed her voice to the point where she became one of the world's greatest contraltos. Italian composer Toscanini was said to have commented that a voice like hers comes only once in a century! King continued in the speech by citing Jesus Christ as the best example of one who overcame nonoptimal circumstances. His parents were not of high social standing or people of wealth . . . not aristocrats or belonging to any prestigious groups.

Dr. King concluded: "Not environment, not heredity, but personal response is the final determining factor in our lives. And herein lies our area of responsibility."

According to Dr. King, your life is what you make it. Education and career development is the responsibility of the individual, not their parents, teachers, or anyone else, though many would claim that heredity and environment can absolve people of responsibility. Although these two entities can affect one's life, the most important factor is our response to challenges that arise. If you prepare yourself academically and experientially through various work situations, you can become whatever you dream. That's the American Dream. I believe the current leadership in America's black community could learn a great deal about effective leadership by studying some of the writings and the real history of Dr. King.

Ignorance: The Reason History Repeats Itself

Historical revisionists don't need to put in any effort if no one cares about history in the first place. Many people find history boring and think that pop culture is much more relevant to citizens today. There certainly is nothing wrong with being up to date on the current social issues that affect our lives, but in order to have the proper perspective on current events, we need to know what happened in the past. For example, it is much easier to understand today's unrest in the Middle East when you know about the establishment of a sovereign Israeli territory in 1948 and the intense turmoil and controversy surrounding the placement of that nation in an unwelcoming environment.

And it is much easier to understand why a 7 to 8 percent unemployment rate today is much worse than a rate like that many years ago, because economists were not nearly as facile as they are currently with manipulating numbers. A good student of history would understand that the labor force participation rate is a more accurate indicator of the level of employment nationwide. That number has been steadily declining since 2009. This indicates that many people are simply giving up on working and as a result are not being counted when calculating the unemployment rate that is widely reported. However, the labor force participation rate captures these individuals and is one of the most accurate reflections of the state of employment. These are just two of many examples of the kinds of things informed citizens should know in order to properly interpret what they read in newspapers or hear on the news networks. Many pundits are all too happy to take advantage of the lack of such knowledge in order to manipulate an unsuspecting populace.

Another excellent reason to be familiar with history is to avoid repeating the same mistakes. The stock market crash of 1929 exacted a severe toll on the people of our nation and our legislators realized, in hindsight, that some of our banking and investment policies had contributed to the crash. Several laws were crafted, including the Glass-Steagall Act, which separated commercial and investment banking activities. Sixty to seventy years later we forgot about many of the horrors of those difficult financial times as well as the reasons why we imposed appropriate regulation on speculative financial activity involving private resources. It only took about twenty years before we faced another near crash. The new regulations that had been put in place were even harsher than the ones that followed the crash of 1929. Perhaps this was an overreaction, but none of it ever had to happen again if our leaders had been more diligent in their study and understanding of history as well as their understanding of human nature, which is characterized by such traits as greed and selfishness. I am not one of those persons who thinks that no regulations are necessary on behalf of the government, but I believe careful attention to history and regular meetings with experts of differing views can provide a great deal of safety and help us avoid unnecessary pain.

We cannot ignore the socially tragic events of our past, but they can be taught in the context of learning experiences that improved our unity and vision. For instance, we were dragged, kicking and screaming, into both world wars because of our isolationist policies. Many of our allies and some of our own citizens were not happy with our reluctance to enter the fray, but we naïvely thought that we could remain neutral and even benefit financially by selling supplies and arms to anyone with money. From these experiences, we learned the importance of putting the fire out before it gets too big. We also learned that isolationist policies are not a luxury to be afforded the pinnacle nation in the world. With power comes great responsibility and the need to lead rather than simply react to volatile international situations with the potential to affect our security. This does not require our involvement with all the international conflicts in the world, but strategic overt or covert intervention can preclude future difficulties. Even as this book is being written, massive demonstrations and horrific fighting is taking place in Egypt where ultimate control remains uncertain. We clearly don't know which side to support in the conflict and it is therefore wise to adopt a wait-and-see attitude. This is a marked contrast to the situation that occurred in Iran four years ago when the populace was rising up against an unjust government and we stood by and did nothing as the people were slaughtered by the military. If we use these occurrences as learning experiences that enhance our future international relationships, it will be worthwhile.

We live in a sophisticated world with many moving parts and it is no longer acceptable or advisable for Americans to know more about the candidates on *Dancing with the Stars* than they do about current affairs and who their representatives are. More important, we can evaluate what we hear in the news and from political candidates only if we are able to put it in the context of historical knowledge. The more we know about the great things that our nation has accomplished, the more pride and patriotism we cultivate among the citizenry.

Action Steps

1. Read some of Dr. Martin Luther King Jr.'s speeches and see if you can determine why he could be considered a conservative.
2. Determine to stay abreast of current events by reading an objective newspaper or watching an objective news broadcast daily. Avoid news sources that leave out major stories because they don't fit a political agenda.

3. Consider whether you have ever suppressed knowledge or arguments that disprove a viewpoint that you hold.

4. If you identify an area where you have revised history or selectively ignored a fact, admit it. Challenge those with whom you disagree to do the same.

5

BIGOTRY

It is sin to despise one's neighbors; blessed are those who help the poor.

PROVERBS 14:21

When my mother, brother, and I returned to Detroit after living in Boston for a couple of years, we moved into a multifamily dwelling in a racially mixed neighborhood. It was the early sixties, I was ten years old, and the civil rights movement was still in its adolescent stages. We lived adjacent to the railroad tracks, which served as the line of demarcation between primarily black and primarily white communities. Since our home was on the white side of the tracks, my brother and I attended Higgins Elementary School, where there were only a handful of black students, most of whom were assigned to the special education section. I was very slight in build, so I was assigned to a regular classroom even though my academic performance was abominable, because the administrators recognized that there was a lot of violence in the special education classrooms and that my size might not be conducive to long-term survival.

Racial stereotyping was common and widely accepted among both adults and children and racially charged comments were often heard.

The black kids were greatly outnumbered in our neighborhood and tended to be rather docile and submissive in order to avoid trouble. On the other side of the tracks there were a number of black gangs that tended to be quite aggressive toward one another and toward whites. There was a community center nearby on the black side of the tracks that was well equipped and attracted youngsters from both communities with its after-school activities. On most days everyone got along at the center, but whenever there was an interracial fight the spectators promptly chose sides based on race. The adult supervisors would intervene quickly, but at times the feelings were so intense that fights between black and white gangs ensued, sometimes with significant injuries.

Although I never joined one of the gangs, I knew a lot of people who were in them and was privy to the conversations of both black and white gang members. Hate speech and animosity were rampant on both sides, with an abundance of derogatory and hateful names being casually tossed about. Because of my religious upbringing and the constant preaching of my mother about God's love and the need to treat everyone equally, I never bought into the race baiting and hatred that I saw all around me. Nevertheless, I became very aware of the negative opinions and inappropriate emotional attitudes in both the black and white communities. I saw black gangs plotting against white individuals in the same way that white groups plotted against black individuals. In other words, the prejudice, hatred, and racism were not exclusive to only one group.

I can vividly remember being the only black student in my eighth-grade math class at Wilson Junior High School in Detroit. We had a substitute math teacher from one of the Slavic countries who just could not comprehend how I was able to constantly achieve the highest math scores on all the tests. She was constantly sending notes home to my mother about the miraculous achievements in my academic endeavors. I seriously doubt that she was a bad person, but she had been fully indoctrinated into the belief that blacks were intellectually inferior, so my success was a miracle in her eyes.

I also remember seeing black kids throwing rocks at Hasidic Jews simply because they dressed differently and because no one was stopping them from engaging in such racist and mean-spirited acts. In retrospect, one of the cruelest things I've ever witnessed was the taunting, teasing, and harassment of elderly people who had difficulty getting around. These are only a few examples of the latent prejudice that exists in our society.

In my experience, bigotry tends to be a product of ignorance. The more sheltered one is, the more likely one is to have negative views about someone who belongs to an unfamiliar group. Areas where bigotry is damaging the unity of American society are race, religion, gender, age, and sexual orientation. Let's look at each of these individually.

Racism

Racial bigotry is certainly much less common in America today than it was when I was growing up. Because segregation was so prevalent, there were not a lot of opportunities for members of different races to work together and socialize together. Since whites held the most powerful and lucrative positions in society, most of them were certainly in no hurry to share those positions with others. Blacks, on the other hand, were becoming progressively more educated and therefore impatient to share the fruits of their labors. This eagerness was frequently misinterpreted by whites who coined the term *uppity* to characterize those blacks who, in their opinion, didn't "know their place." Those blacks who were very docile and cooperative were frequently rewarded with better jobs and more money, while the less subservient blacks were humiliated and disrespected.

It was common for whites to believe that blacks were dirty, unintelligent, and sexually promiscuous. These beliefs informed hiring practices and property distribution. Many of the whites in those days found ways to rationalize their unjust treatment of fellow human beings, arguing that they were not racists but rather protectors of traditional values. It wasn't unusual for some whites to say that blacks should be grateful to have been brought out of the African jungles where they faced a very meager existence. (Talk about historical revisionism and elitism, especially since the lives of blacks in Africa were complete; they had knowledge of how to live off the land, something that American whites of that time would probably have had difficulty doing if they were placed there.)

Unfortunately, blacks also harbored some false assumptions about whites. As a youngster I frequently heard that white people carried lice and that you had to be very careful when you were around them or you would get them too. It was also frequently said that whites were greedy and cruel. Obviously, none of the things that were said about either group were true, but these kinds of bigoted notions were passed down through the generations, thereby poisoning race relations.

Though the days of legalized segregation are over, racist bigotry and prejudice still exist today, both in overt and covert ways. I can remember times when I would be walking in a white neighborhood and in short order a police car would show up, undoubtedly summoned by a concerned onlooker. Unfortunately, this and worse still happens today, as evidenced by the Trayvon Martin case. A neighborhood watchman, George Zimmerman, suspicious of the young black man who was walking through the neighborhood late at night, shot and killed Martin after an altercation. The real tragedy is that a young life was lost and another life ruined because both individuals made assumptions about the other that were probably untrue. I hope this tragedy is not useless and we can learn something about how neighborhood watchpersons should be trained by police and what types of weapons, if any, they should use. I love the idea of tasers for neighborhood guardians, because they usually are not lethal.

More subtle than assuming someone to be a criminal because of his or her race, expecting someone to vote a certain way or follow a certain philosophical line of thinking simply due to skin color is every bit as outrageous and unfair as Jim Crow laws. To facilitate dependency by giving able-bodied people handouts rather than requiring they work for pay is every bit as cruel (even if unintentionally so) as the activities practiced by racists of the past. If the guilty parties could exercise enough humility to recognize that they might actually be doing harm to those they purport to help, I'm certain that things could be done fairly quickly and in cooperation with others of goodwill to improve the plight of millions of Americans.

Religious Bigotry

Religious bigotry is also a problem today. While we might think we only see it in the streets of Iran or Egypt, and congratulate ourselves for being extremely tolerant when it comes to religious freedom, we still need to make progress in this area. A close look at our attitudes nationally reveals a drastic need for improvement in our understanding of religious tolerance as a fundamental pillar of the American Constitution.

It is widely believed that throughout history more people have been killed in the name of religious causes than any other cause. Often religious crusaders are so certain that only they can be right, that they will stop at nothing to either convert others or eliminate them. Certainly the Islamic extremists of today feel that way, just as the Christian crusaders felt years ago. This history of intolerance by some religious adherents has understandably caused many people to shun religion and to look unfavorably upon those seen as religious.

As a Christian, I can fully understand the aversion to religious extremism and hypocritical religious propaganda put in place to create wealth and maintain positions of a very few leaders. Jesus Christ would also have an aversion to this kind of false religion. He preached love, acceptance, and forgiveness. Even though he was all-powerful, he led a humble life directed toward improving the lot of others, but the Christian movement that he started has been so distorted by some that it is sometimes hard to recognize.

If one is able to cut through all the garbage and analyze the real principles set forth by Christ, they can be distilled into two major entities: love of God and love of your neighbor. That means respecting what God has told us and being caretakers of all He has created. And it also means being respectful of every man and being fair to all people regardless of how they may differ from you. It means leaving the judging to God and not trying to impose our ideological beliefs on others. This last point is one that is particularly important for those entering the political arena and who may at some point assume power.

Whether or not one likes Christianity or any other religion is not the point, however. Our Constitutional Bill of Rights states that "Congress can make no law respecting an establishment of religion, or prohibiting the free exercise thereof." In other words, our government should not support particular denominations or religious groups, but neither should it prevent anyone from expressing their religion.

Unfortunately, our nation seems to have forgotten the latter part of that statement. The media is peppered with stories about communities or organizations demanding the removal of patriotic symbols or crosses from private property simply because such symbols are offensive to some. Recently a community in the Northeast was forced to remove a memorial to fallen soldiers because the memorial was reminiscent of a Christmas tree. In this case the bias was so great against the concept of Christmas that it trumped respect and honor for our fallen military personnel.

In the rotunda of the original Johns Hopkins Hospital is a twelve-foot statue of Jesus beckoning those in need to come to him. When that statue was first placed, several physicians and scientists vehemently protested its presence, stating that Hopkins was a scientific institution and there was no room for religious symbols. The controversy grew so ferocious that the decision was made to remove the statue. Ironically, the protest against the removal of the statue was even more vehement and the statue was brought back and has remained in that location to this day.

As upsetting as religious bigotry is in the private sphere, it is an even more serious concern in our government. There is nothing in our Constitution that supports the banning of manger scenes or other signs of Christmas in public places, yet some have called for their removal. For example, at Palisades Park in Santa Monica, California, manger scenes had been on display every Christmas for over fifty years, but they were banned in 2012. And this type of intolerance is proliferating throughout the country.

The fact that some people want to take the words *under God* out of the "Pledge of Allegiance" and others want to remove the words *In God we trust* from our money, demonstrates the depth of misunderstanding of the First Amendment's separation clause. The spirit of religious freedom supports various kinds of religious expression, and instead of trying to restrict one group or another from celebrating their religious beliefs through symbolism, we should be encouraging free expression on behalf of every group.

Totalitarianism always starts with restrictions on the rights of others. We must avoid this at all costs. George Washington even said, "If the freedom of speech is taken away, then dumb and silent we may be led, like sheep to the slaughter."

It is appalling how far our country has strayed from the

principles of the founding fathers. In Michigan, in 2013, a high school banned its football team from praying on the field. The practice of team members opting to pray together was started when one of the students had requested that the team pray for an ill family member after a game. The ten-year-old tradition was banned because of "concern" by the family of a current team member who brought the practice to the attention of the ACLU. And in Washington, the capital of our country, our congresspeople are not allowed to say "Merry Christmas" in their mail unless they pay for the postage out of their own pockets. The Congressional Franking Committee, which reviews all mail, will not "frank" (send free of charge) any congressperson's mail that has "Merry Christmas" or any other holiday greeting in it.

These are examples of the kind of bias that ignores the rights and freedom of those who disagree with the purveyors of prejudice. The bias exists on both sides of the political spectrum as demonstrated by the horrible things the Christian Right said about Bill Clinton because of his affair with a White House intern, when in fact several Republican leaders were also engaged in extramarital adventurism. It would probably be a good thing for both sides to stay out of private issues that don't affect one's duties. Many on the Right exhibit bigotry by assuming that those who believe in the sacredness of big government programs have socialistic tendencies. This is of course not true and many people who have grown up with significant government assistance simply don't know any other way of life and are patriotic American citizens. We all need to take a deep breath and concentrate on educating the populace about true liberty and justice while respecting one another's religious—or nonreligious—beliefs. No one's religious beliefs should have to be hidden in a truly free and open society, but if we the people do not stand up against the religious bigotry that exists right now, we may end up without any religious freedom at all.

Sexism

Sexist bigotry is another problem, despite the tremendous strides we have made toward achieving equality of the sexes in America. I can easily remember when people were shocked to see a female commercial airline pilot or executive in a large organization. Female surgeons were almost unheard of when I was a child. Today more than half of the medical students in America are female and the chiefs of surgery at many large institutions, including Johns Hopkins, are women. As was the case with blacks, once people had an opportunity to work closely with members of the opposite sex, it became readily apparent that they were just as competent as anyone else.

Nevertheless, there remain in our society people who doubt the ability of women to be good police officers, firefighters, or military combatants. They claim that women are too weak for such jobs. Anyone who is truly objective would have to admit that there are many men who are too weak for such jobs and there would be no rationale for putting such men in those positions just as there is no rationale for putting such women in those positions. On the other hand, there are many women who are stronger than most men and can easily handle these roles. We need to start evaluating people based on their abilities and not on their sex or other congenital characteristics.

Keep in mind that not all the sexist bias is directed toward one gender. In recent years, sitcoms and commercials have portrayed men, particularly fathers, as buffoons. People seem to derive great pleasure from mocking men's foolishness while extolling women's wisdom and cleverness. While they may feel that this type of sexism is fine because there was discrimination against women for so many years, this is a childish mentality. Both men and women should be treated with dignity and respect. When men and women are able to work together as equals by bringing their specific skills and talents to the table, a type of synergy develops that can be beneficial to everyone.

Ageism

Ageism is another form of bigotry today. In the early 1900s, the average age of death in America was less than fifty years. Now that mark is approaching eighty years of age. As a result, we are seeing larger numbers of elderly individuals in our society. I sometimes observe younger people acting quite impatient when they are behind an elderly individual who is moving slowly up a ramp or flight of stairs. Instead of showing disrespect, these young people need to think about the fact that they, too, one day will be relegated to the slow lane and will be appreciative of patience by others.

Younger people need to realize that the opportunities they have today exist largely because of the hard work and sacrifices of those who preceded them. Certainly we would not enjoy the kind of freedom we have today if our ancestors had not valiantly fought and defeated the axis powers of World War II. Not only should we be thankful to the brave men who fought and died for our sakes but we should remember the millions of women who occupied the vacancies in the factories created by the military draft. From their strength and determination were created more airplanes, tanks, and mortars than anyone could have imagined, thus supplying the fuel for military victory. As a mark of respect, we should be more than happy to care for these elders who have done so much for us.

On the flip side, many older people have negative impressions of younger people and their work ethic, or their use of drugs, and their musical selections. If they stimulate their memory banks they will discover that when they were young, older people said some similar things about them. Of course we all have biases based on where we are in the stages of life. Wisdom gives the kind of perspective that allows one to appreciate others wherever they are along life's journey.

It is also important for the generation in power currently to realize that it has an obligation to the next generations, which if unfulfilled will likely create a level of animosity toward them that is unprecedented. Thomas Jefferson said it was immoral to leave debt to the next generation. He would be speechless if he were resurrected today and saw that we are leaving the next generation a $17 trillion national debt. If the next generations were paying closer attention, it is likely that they would be protesting the unbridled borrowing against their future. The stark reality is that if we don't immediately assume fiscal responsibility and adopt policies that are conducive to economic growth, an economic disaster will ensue that will affect all generations. This is another area where a little common sense will go a long way.

Homophobia

Finally, there's the issue of bigotry regarding sexual orientation. As I stated earlier, people who have differing opinions about gay marriage are likely to always exist. There has been a long and shameful history of gay bashing in America that thankfully is waning. However, this bigotry can still be seen in the assumption by many on the Right that gays should not have access to children because they are more likely to commit rape or engage in aberrant sexual indoctrination. If this is true, it should be relatively easy to prove statistically, but such proof has yet to be provided.

Unfortunately, the mantle of hatred has been taken up by the other side, which feels that hateful speech and actions toward anyone who doesn't embrace the gay agenda is justified. Obviously hatred on either side of the opinion ledger is unacceptable and should be shunned by all.

Defeating Bigotry

Unless we are able to apply both condemnation and praise equally and objectively, we will do nothing except exacerbate the social relationships that are vital to a healthy society. The problems facing America are so overwhelming that we can ill afford to expend energy on issues stimulated by bigotry of any type. Unless we are able to focus on the big-picture items, like many societies before us, we will be agents of our own destruction. I strongly believe that if we adhere to the creed "one nation, under God, indivisible with liberty and justice for all," that we can avoid the pitfalls that have so effectively disabled the pinnacle nations that preceded us. Let us live the words, rather than just allow them to roll off our tongues without thinking.

Action Steps

1. When ready to call someone a nasty name, stop and evaluate the situation from that person's point of view.
2. Stand up for the rights of someone with whom you disagree.
3. Identify an area where you have participated in bigotry and plan two concrete actions you can take this week to remedy the situation.
4. Be aware of bigotry shown toward you and plan two concrete ways to civilly confront the bigots.

6

NO WINNERS IN POLITICAL FIGHTING

A troublemaker plants seeds of strife; gossip separates the best of friends.

PROVERBS 16:28

I worked as a supervisor of highway cleanup crews around the Detroit area during the summers of 1970 and 1971. Mostly from inner-city Detroit, the young men in these crews were not overly ambitious and enjoyed having a good time. At first they were always interested in knowing the minimum amount of work required of them in order to be paid. They were quite clever in devising schemes that would meet that minimum requirement without exerting excessive effort.

Since they were particularly averse to working long hours in the hot sun, I proposed a framework that would allow them to do the bulk of their work early in the morning before rising temperatures made work unpleasant. Instead of paying them by the hour, I would pay them for a full day's work when they had collected a certain amount of trash. Prior to such an offer, they each worked independently while surreptitiously keeping an eye on how much work was being done by the others. Now they became more insistent on efficiency and the best way to quickly complete the work. They devised methods of working together, which greatly enhanced not only their efficiency but their satisfaction. Working faster and more effectively than any other crews became a badge of pride for them and they actually looked forward to their work, while at the same time establishing very cordial working relationships with one another. There were occasional days when dissension arose in the ranks and on those days there was a noticeable decline in the crew's effectiveness. If an outside force wanted to lessen the effectiveness of a crew, they would sow seeds of discord, and simply watch them grow.

The work crew mirrors the political landscape in our country. When working toward the common goal of American people's welfare, Republicans and Democrats get along relatively well. Even though they have philosophical differences they are able to work together to pass legislation that is beneficial for everyone. When special interest groups influence one side or the other, creating dissension, Congress doesn't work well at all. Unfortunately, polarizing influences—such as unions that want what they want, gay rights groups, isolationists, and others who cannot or will not consider the opinions of others—have become stronger in recent years, robbing from the pool of moderate legislators and increasing the numbers of extreme legislators. Their efforts explain why it is so difficult to come to consensus on almost anything.

"My Way or the Highway"

Washington, DC, is dysfunctional today because the primary
two political parties have become opponents instead of teammates with different approaches to the same goal. In a speech
not long ago, President Obama referred to the Republicans as
enemies. While it was wrong of him to refer to them as such,
many of the party probably see themselves as his enemies, largely
because of the Affordable Care Act, the biggest governmental
program in the history of the United States, which was passed
without a single Republican vote in the House or the Senate.
Never before has any major society-changing piece of legislation
been passed in this country without bipartisan effort. During the
bill's passage, I had an opportunity to speak with one of the
president's senior staffers and said that this unilateral act would
create an unprecedented level of dissension and rancor that could
preclude cordial working relationships for an extended period of
time. The response I got was "So what? That's nothing new."

This "my way or the highway" approach has resulted in disaster. Influenced by special interest groups, like some of the
insurance companies that stood to benefit from the exchanges if
they worked well, the Trial Lawyers Association, which supports
anything that doesn't include tort reform, and many liberal universities, which blindly support anything disguised in the mantle
of liberalism, Democrats tried to create a bandwagon effect to
alleviate any anxiety felt by the public. But by rushing to pass the
bill while they still controlled the House and Senate, the Democrats passed a program so massive that many components of it
have not even been tested. As Nancy Pelosi once famously said,
"We have to pass it, so we can see what's in it."

As we are finding out what's in it, more groups, including labor unions that originally supported it, are withdrawing their support. A program that was supposed to reduce costs and allow people to keep their insurance if they wanted to, is raising costs and making it impractical for people to keep their previous insurance. It is also rapidly expanding the number of part-time workers in our country because the law does not require employers to provide health care insurance for part-time workers. The result will funnel almost everybody into government health care.

Although some of the Democrats may have felt temporary joy when they passed the bill, in the long run, they destroyed harmony. The Democrats now have an albatross around their necks with Obamacare and will forever be blamed for destroying a reasonable health care system that needed improvement, but was working for 85 percent of the populace. The Republicans were shut out of the process and have been largely marginalized, and they continue to weaken themselves with internal squabbling. Everyone loses when our politicians and our people engage in this kind of political infighting.

I can remember a time when senators and congresspeople from different political parties were friends and happily worked together to help our nation prosper. In recent years politicians have capitulated to divisive forces that drive wedges into every crack and then hype the differences of opinion to force each side deep into their ideological corners, making it difficult to compromise without appearing to surrender. A prime example is the federal budget battles we seem to face annually. They have become games of brinksmanship where both parties participate in a game of chicken. The goal is not to solve problems but rather to pin on opponents the blame for lack of progress or for a government shutdown. Those representatives who play this game rather than represent the will of their constituencies should be voted out of office regardless of their party affiliation, and should be replaced by people who understand the dangers of fiscal irresponsibility and moral decay.

Many of our politicians seem to relish their role as dividers today. It is essential to the viability of a united nation that we learn to recognize their tactics and resist. If we are fragmented, we cannot provide a united response to tyranny, and we certainly cannot get things done effectively.

Division Tactics

A favorite tactic of dividers is the demonization of their opponents. It is rare for them to engage in a rational conversation but they are eager, particularly when surrounded by people of like mind, to viciously castigate those with opposing views. Usually the questionable motive they ascribe to their victim is the very same thing they are guilty of themselves. It is sometimes tempting to get into the mud pit with them and hurl insults, but this serves to lower one to their level and accomplishes nothing. For instance, recently a prominent congresswoman stated that it was not possible to cut one penny from the federal budget, and implied that those advocating this were heartless. The sad thing is that anyone who thinks at all knows that this is not true, but they are more loyal to their party than to truth or the well-being of future generations.

Another tactic of the dividers is to hold up one of their own as an example of someone who has been treated unjustly in some fashion, and say that this is what their opponents want to do to everyone. Last year, Democrats claimed that a Georgetown law student was poorly treated by those who did not wish to make free birth control pills available to her. Not only did they say that Republicans discriminated against her by refusing to pay for her birth control but they suggested that this refusal meant the Republicans were engaged in a "war on women." The argument had very little substance or truth but was nearly wholly focused on victimization and blame.

Demagoguery is another tool of dividers. Dividers on both sides of the aisle make sweeping and often obviously false statements about their opponents, recognizing that most people understand that this is foolishness, but a growing number don't think for themselves and blindly trust their political leaders, believing everything they say. These gullible voters believe emotionally manipulative arguments presented by strong leaders, especially when the arguments are repeated frequently and are not called into question by most of the media.

Yet another device used by the dividers is quoting their opponents out of context. The extreme media uses this technique frequently and when they are caught, they simply say "My bad" and quickly move on. All of these techniques are designed to call into question their opponent's character and set them up as enemies of the people who should be resisted on every level. It is my fervent hope and prayer that "the people" will soon awaken and recognize that they are being manipulated by real enemies—those who are constantly trying to divide us and make us believe that we are one another's enemies.

"We the People" or "They the Government"?

Over the course of time many Americans have forgotten that "we the people" are actually at the top of the food chain as far as authority is concerned in this nation. The Republicans don't run our nation. The Democrats don't run our nation. We do. However, by dividing and engaging in political squabbles, we have allowed the government to grow so large and powerful that it has now become the boss, progressively taking charge of all of our lives. It has reached the size where it is incredibly dangerous for one half of the dividers to take control, since they can then wreak havoc on the lives of those who oppose them.

For example, the IRS targeted Tea Party organizations for intense scrutiny and unfair treatment. To add insult to injury, the head of the IRS pleaded the Fifth Amendment rather than answer questions about her involvement in the scandal. Other government officials have said they had adequately investigated the problem and were sure no one in the government's executive branch knew anything about the decision to persecute American citizens. However, congressional testimony has subsequently revealed that the offending agents did receive instructions from higher-ups in Washington.

What can we do about this type of situation? In times like this, the people must understand their power and their responsibility. This means getting together in groups like early citizens of this country did, discussing the problems and working together to put pressure on their elected representatives to use all available legal avenues to flush out the truth and punish the culprits. If illegal actions by dividers are just allowed to fade away with little or no consequences, we can be guaranteed to have repeat performances and significant exacerbations of this kind of abuse.

In the 2012 presidential election, tens of millions of Americans did not vote even though they were eligible to do so. I have had an opportunity to talk to thousands of such people who have become so discouraged and disillusioned by the bickering of their representatives that they have simply given up on our nation and its promise to be centered on the people. I encourage those people to fight rather than give up, but this should be a fight for unity, not for a party. If Americans simply choose to vote for the person who has a *D* or an *R* by their name, we will get what we deserve, which is what we have now.

I would love it if party labels were not allowed on ballots and people were forced to actually know who they were voting for. Blind loyalty to a party platform is tantamount to relinquishing the important duties of intelligent voting. Leaders of both parties want to have voters who will blindly follow them and not even consider what's being said by their opponents. This was not the intention of the multiparty system. Rather it was to make sure that different sides of the issues were carefully examined, allowing the average citizen to then make an intelligent choice. I believe that it would be beneficial to the future of our nation to find ways to increase the likelihood that voters would actually know about the person for whom they are voting, rather than their party affiliation.

Strength in Unity

In 1968 I was a diehard Detroit Tigers baseball fan. I listened to almost every game and could tell you quite a bit about each of the players. That year the Tigers won the American League pennant for the first time in thirty-seven years, which resulted in great unity across racial and socioeconomic barriers throughout the city. Even more remarkable was the team spirit that created almost miraculous comebacks in what appeared to be impossible situations. Every night there was a different hero and the esprit de corps was magical. The World Series was played against the St. Louis Cardinals, who amassed a three-games-to-one lead. Although things looked grim for the Tigers, no one in Detroit was willing to give up on them, because of the incredible comebacks they had witnessed all season long. Because of that unity and belief in one another, and the backing of the fans, the team won the last three games, taking the World Series crown in seven games. Anyone who does not believe in the power of unity certainly did not experience the 1968 Detroit Tigers.

That same kind of unity is possible among the people of our nation with the right kind of leadership. But we the people must for ourselves determine that we will be indivisible regardless of the leadership, and we must exercise our ability to identify the divisive forces and vote them out of office.

If we are to put an end to division, people from all political persuasions will have to stop fighting one another and seek true unity, not just a consensus that benefits one party. Right now, some of the Democrats say, "We all want to help people," but their next sentence is about how Republicans want people to die. One Democratic representative famously said, "The Republican health plan is for people to die quickly." Republicans, on the other hand, often talk about how Democrats want to change America into a socialist country. They may not intend to sow seeds of discord but the constant spewing of hatred is having a deleterious effect on the unity of the nation. The America haters and extremists may not be that concerned about the well-being of the country, but reasonable people from both political parties must be able to see the big picture and not fall into the traps set by those who wish to divide and conquer. We must be able to sit down and engage in civil discussion without casting aspersions on others.

Action Steps

1. Pretend that you are in a different political party from yours and that you must give a rational defense of something you currently strongly disagree with that the other party embraces.
2. Ask the people who spend the most time around you to let you know if and when you are being intolerant.
3. Determine to study at least two alternatives to the Affordable Care Act.
4. Invite friends and neighbors over for a civil political discussion.

7

ENSLAVING OUR CHILDREN—
DON'T SELL THE FUTURE

Good people leave an inheritance to their grandchildren, but
the sinner's wealth passes to the godly.

PROVERBS 13:22

I have a lot of very wealthy friends and have watched with interest over the years how they raised their children. One family
I knew always provided their several children with the best of
everything including limousine drivers and top-of-the-line
clothing. There was always an abundance of maids, gardeners,
and other people to care for personal needs. Unforeseen circumstances abruptly ended their life of luxury and no significant inheritance was left for the children. If they had lived a
slightly less extravagant lifestyle and put away a small fraction
of their enormous income each month, the tragic event would
not have had such a profound effect on their lives. Living large
and disregarding the future was a major mistake for this family,
and it continues to be a predominant issue for today's families
from all socioeconomic groups.

Unfortunately today in America, many parents appear to be more concerned about their own lifestyles than the financial landscape they are leaving behind for those who will follow us. Our national debt, which is the accumulation of annual federal budget deficits, is now approaching $17 trillion with a trajectory that could take us well beyond $20 trillion within the next few years. These astronomical numbers represent new financial landmines unlike anything we have encountered previously. We do not know what the result of this kind of debt will be, but it can't possibly be good!

Debt Leads to Disaster

There are recent examples of what happens to nations that continue to accumulate debt without regard to its consequences. Like ancient Rome, modern Greece continued to expand the dole for all citizens while increasing taxes on businesses and doing nothing to foster the economy's growth. As it became clear to lending nations that this pattern was continuing with no imposition of fiscal responsibility, they became less willing to make additional loans to the Greek government, precipitating a crisis. As the Greek government worked to cut down on spending, Greek citizens rioted in the streets to protest austerity measures that decreased the monies they felt they were entitled to receive from the government.

It is hard to believe that our leaders in both political parties do not understand that they are jeopardizing the financial future of the next generations by allowing continued debt accumulation, even if they are slowing the rise of that debt. The government recently announced it will pay down our debt by

$35 billion in the next quarter. This sounds good, but that equals about 0.02 percent of the total amount owed. They will probably pat themselves on the back and proclaim what a great job they are doing while at the same time borrowing even more during the next quarter rather than continuing the downward trend in borrowing.

Our Ballooning Debt

Here are some interesting facts of the last few years, demonstrating how exponentially the problem is increasing: In 2007 the United States federal debt was 64 percent of the gross domestic product (GDP). By 2012, the federal debt had risen to 103 percent of GDP. It is still growing, although admittedly at a slower pace. The implementation of Obamacare and the progressive aging of the populace at large will do nothing to help these numbers.

And as of March 19, 2012, the national debt had increased more during the three years and two months of the current administration than during the eight years of the previous administration. Anyone with a modicum of common sense can see that this is a huge problem and that whoever downplays it or uses rosy language to assuage the anxiety of the populace is disingenuous at best.

Many, particularly in the Democratic Party, seem to feel that this level of debt is not a serious problem because the U.S. government has the ability to print money. Unfortunately, this solution cannot be sustained indefinitely because the more money we print, the more we devalue the dollar, thereby gradually weakening our financial foundation. Since Franklin D. Roosevelt decoupled the U.S. dollar from gold, our currency has been backed only by our good name. Not only has this resulted in fiscal policy problems, but it has also steadily increased the gap between the wealth of the rich and poor in this country and provided the opportunity to do a lot of fancy currency manipulation. Nothing good will happen if we continue along this reckless course of fiscal irresponsibility.

Economic Growth as a Solution

I believe there is some relatively painless budget cutting that can be done, because there is a fat layer in virtually every governmental budget, but the real emphasis should be on growing the economy, which has been extremely sluggish for the last several years. I have great respect for economists and their complex theories, but I don't believe sophisticated theories are necessary to spur economic growth in our country. We have the highest corporate tax rates in the world, which obviously encourage many U.S. companies to conduct business outside of America. We also have high individual taxation rates and high rates for small businesses. None of this is conducive to economic growth, particularly during times that resemble a recession.

Couple this with excessive governmental interference in business and the imposition of a national health care program that adds substantially to the cost of each employee and you have a formula for persistent anemic growth. If the rest of the world, and especially China, loses confidence in America's ability to handle its fiscal responsibilities and calls for repayment of the money we owe them, an unimaginable economic crisis would likely ensue.

Ignore the "Spiders"

When I was nine or ten years old, some friends and I were climbing a rock mountain located in Franklin Park in the Roxbury section of Boston. We felt we were invincible and paid little attention to the signs forbidding such activities. I had climbed those rocks on many occasions and really didn't even consider the possible consequences of falling—death or great bodily harm. This particular day, I was very high on the rock face when the ledge I was standing on broke, leaving me dangling with my hands tightly gripping the protruding rocks. At that point I realized that my life was in danger and it was my own fault. I earnestly prayed to God asking Him to save me and promising that I would never engage in such stupid activities again. Suddenly off to my right, I saw a cubbyhole large enough to admit my hand, providing me a better position from which I could place my feet and continue my climb. I have never been a fan of big, hairy wolf spiders and the cubbyhole featured a nest of them, but considering the alternatives, they looked like beautiful, welcoming creatures and I happily placed my hand in their domain. Gaining that leverage, I was able to complete my ascension to the top of the mountain for the very last time. I was never even tempted to climb it again.

Our government reminds me of myself in this story as it pushes its debts higher and higher, ignoring the warning signs posted by history. Feeling invincible, it brushes off concerns about the fragility of financial markets easily panicked by rumors as a result of the vulnerability created by debt. It ignores the U.S. Constitution, our chief warning sign, which describes the responsibilities of the government toward the people, attempting to preclude a massive and intrusive governing structure that would require so much spending.

If we fail to heed these warnings, unexpected disaster will leave us desperately grasping for solutions. Eventually, something is going to slip. Just as entering the domain of the spiders was not a pleasant option for me as a child, adopting a policy of fiscal responsibility is an unpleasant option for our government, which seems to have difficulty distinguishing needs from wants, but there will be no other option.

The difference between my story and the government's situation today is that I learned my lesson after I was miraculously spared, while our government seems incapable of understanding the danger ahead. The debt burden it is creating will have to be paid by someone at some point in time. When we look at history, we see that the ancient Greeks had a complex and large governmental structure that necessitated an ever-growing tax burden on the populace, eventually reducing many of them to serfdom. Although the serf-like population was provided with certain handouts by the state, it was essentially rendered into slaves to the government. Are we in the process of doing the very same thing even though we have examples from the past of the consequences of such a direction?

I do not doubt the sincerity of individuals in both political parties who want to use government to enhance the lives of the citizenry, but I seriously doubt their understanding of our nation's founding principles. We the people need the application of smelling salts to awaken us from a slumber that imperils the financial freedom of the next generations. Only through careful analysis of what is going on today and comparison of today's events with the things that have gone on in societies that preceded us, will we be able to recognize and correct our course. We are engaged in nothing less than a war of philosophies, one of which will lead to prosperity and continued freedom, and the other, which will lead to fundamental changes in who we are and our role in the world. We get to decide which of these futures we want to leave to our children, but we only have a short time to make that decision.

A Balanced Budget

Balancing the budget is not a goal out of reach. The last time the United States experienced an annual budgetary surplus instead of a deficit was during the Clinton administration, when the House of Representatives was controlled by budgetary hawks and the White House was controlled by a president who was pragmatic and not an ideologue. Even though Democrats and Republicans had different ideas regarding fiscal policy, they were not so entrenched in their positions that they couldn't understand the other side and compromise. If that spirit of cooperation had continued with multiple years of budgetary surpluses, by now we would have had a much smaller national debt or perhaps as in 1835, no national debt at all, as occurred under the watch of President Andrew Jackson.

Although our financial problems may seem large and complex, there is nothing about them that is not subject to commonsense solutions. The question is are we willing to abandon ideological gridlock and learn to compromise for the sake of those who follow us in this nation? Also, do we know the meaning of the word *sacrifice* anymore, and if not, are we willing to learn what that word means and to enact policies that are truly compassionate toward our progeny? We have time to do it if we are willing to act now before the crisis occurs.

If we spend our money wisely, we can still be quite comfortable without stressing about budgetary shortfalls. We don't even have to be heartless when it comes to reducing the size of government, even though those who promoted such massive growth were not particularly caring regarding our long-term financial well-being. If we simply do not replace those workers who retire, natural attrition will quickly work in our favor. It might be necessary to retrain and shift some younger workers into areas that need them, but the result will be the same: a slow shrinking of government bloat. These kinds of simple and compassionate solutions cannot only make a big difference in the budget but will improve the esprit de corps.

During the recent sequester and government shutdown, the executive branch of government, which has the power to decide where to focus the budgetary cuts, made little or no attempt to target the cuts in such a way that they would have a minimal effect on the population at large. Whatever the reasons for this lack of compassionate effort, maturation on both sides of the political aisle should lead politicians to more intelligent budgetary solutions. Everyone knows there is waste and duplication in virtually every federal program. To deny this is a complete divorce from reality. Nevertheless, there are those who insist on continually raising the federal debt ceiling and consequently the federal debt. The directors of every federal program know where the excesses are and if directed to cut a certain small percentage of their budget, could do so without wreaking havoc on the program and its beneficiaries. In order to be fair, the argument should not be about which programs to cut, but rather about what percentage gets trimmed from every federal program with no sacred cows. Such cuts should be made every year until we eliminate the federal budget deficit.

The people who should be the most concerned about our growing national debt and our future obligations are the young people in our society who will be saddled with massive taxes if we don't alter our course. When I was in college, students were much more involved in what was going on in the country and there were frequent marches and protests. Other than the misguided Occupy Wall Street movement, there has been very little heard from the next generation about current fiscal issues. It is essential for the next generation of young people to start paying closer attention to what is going on in our country and in the world because it will profoundly affect their future. They need to make their voices heard in order to create some guilt among the members of my generation who are greedily spending their future resources.

Action Steps

1. Try to live for one week without accumulating any additional debt.
2. Calculate how long it would take to pay off a national debt of $17 trillion if we pay $1 billion per day with no further deficit spending. This does not begin to address the over $90 trillion in unfunded liabilities associated

with entitlements. Determine which candidates in the next election would take quickest action to reduce the debt.

3. Discuss fiscal responsibility with a young person in your sphere of influence this month.

4. When you engage in your next financial endeavor, ask yourself, "How will this affect the next generation?"

PART TWO

—

SOLUTIONS

PUSHING BACK

If you fail under pressure your strength is not very great. Rescue those who are unjustly sentenced to death; don't stand back and let them die. Don't try to avoid responsibility by saying you didn't know about it. For God knows all hearts, and He sees you. He keeps watch over your soul, and He knows you knew! And He will judge all people according to what they have done.

PROVERBS 24:10-12

When I was in middle school in Detroit, school life was reasonably peaceful except for the existence of bullies. There was one particular young man whom I will call Jonathan, who took great delight in beating me and pushing me around as well as heaping verbal abuse on me and others. It reached a point where I would alter my pathways in order to avoid him. I tried to stay out of his sight as much as possible and generally kept very quiet when he was around. One day on the way home from school, he began picking on me for no reason and I simply decided that I had had enough and I challenged him to a fight. He did not wish to fight and decided to leave me alone, not only on that day, but every day after. The situation could have ended up quite differently with my taking a severe beating, but even if that had been the case, I had decided that I would withstand as many beatings as necessary to make it clear that I would no longer be his punching bag.

Even after Jonathan stopped bothering me, there were others to take his place, but that all ended soon after I joined the ROTC in the latter part of the tenth grade and rapidly rose through the ranks. My uniform was covered with ribbons, medals, and ropes that were quite impressive and the bullies had so much respect for that uniform that they showed me great deference.

Today, we Americans may feel bullied by the PC police, elites, historical revisionists, bigots, dividers, and spenders mentioned in the previous sections. We may be discouraged or afraid, but we must take action. As I learned from my experience with Jonathan, there are two ways of dealing with bullies: standing up to them and gaining their respect. Being quiet or trying to ignore them usually doesn't work and frequently emboldens them to keep trying to get a reaction from the victim. Taking calm, mature, rational action is the only way to stop them.

Media Bullies

One of the biggest bullies is the media, which has a tremendous advantage because of the regular platform from which it launches attacks against victims who don't have a national broadcast stage to disseminate their defense. Like Jonathan, the media will continue its relentless attacks on those it does not approve of until they submit or mount a credible counterattack. It is rare that its victims have an equally loud microphone to refute the accusations leveled by their attackers. This means the victims must take maximum advantage of every weapon they do have.

Social media provides one very effective way to gain allies against the media bullies. These allies can help one another collectively recall blatantly untrue positions that have been advocated by the bullies in the past. They can also help organize boycotts of the offending media outlets once a critical mass of individuals has been convinced of the problem. Members of the media are very sensitive to ratings and their behavior can be changed by a strong group of individuals with a large following who threaten to boycott them. If social media is used to persuade large numbers of people to stop watching an offending program, the program's ratings, which determine whether the program will continue, will fall. In the end, most members of the media are more concerned about survival than ideology and will listen when the boycotts are successful, even though they will not admit that the ratings resulted in the changes they subsequently made.

Political Bullies

Politicians are even more sensitive than the media to organized resistance. They count on the fact that most people are not paying close attention to their votes and their actions and frequently are clueless regarding whether their representatives actually reflect their values. They know that many people go into the voting booth looking for a name that looks familiar or one that is affiliated with their political party and simply vote on that basis with no further critical analysis. When well-organized groups within their constituency begin to point out to others their critical shortfallings, they start to panic and will frequently put out television or radio ads trying to reassure voters that they are on their side.

It is hoped and anticipated by the current administration, as well as previous administrations, that the majority of American citizens will be much more interested in what their professional sports teams are doing than they will be in holding leaders accountable. The current crop of politicians and many of those who preceded them are not necessarily bad people, but they believe that they know what is best for people and act on their beliefs rather than fulfilling their role of service to them. By stonewalling and depending on the short memory and attention span of the average citizen, it is quite possible for them to skate by with no consequences for their transgressions.

The way to push back against such officials is to track their votes and demonstrate a consistent voting pattern that is not in the interest of their constituencies. Exposing the negative pattern to the public using social media, radio and television ads, and newspaper articles can wake up apathetic voters and inspire them to take action. The side using this strategy most effectively is likely to be victorious, which means the majority can actually lose if they just sit by and assume that voters will check the records themselves.

As the opposition, we have to be just as persistent as the supporters of the representatives who truly do not represent their constituents. By that I am referring to the people who say one thing to get elected, but then follow the dictates of party leaders rather than the people's will. As I said earlier, I would love to one day see elections in America where we do not indicate party affiliations on the ballot. This would force people to actually research the candidates and make intelligent choices. Until then, we must push back hard to inform our fellow citizens of problems with our leaders.

Citizens also have to be organized enough to keep records of their representatives' responsiveness so they can vote them out of office if necessary. It would be amazing how responsive representatives would become if this were done on a regular basis. What I am talking about is not complex, but does require real energy and willingness to fight for a truly free society. It has been done before: American farmworkers and environmentalists were able to get the toxic pesticide azinphos-methyl (AZM), a chemical warfare agent, removed from the agricultural market through persistent lobbying that led to legal action. Today we need to follow the example of those Americans and heed the words of cultural anthropologist Margaret Mead, who said, "Never doubt that a small group of thoughtful, committed citizens can change the world; indeed, it's the only thing that ever has."

Academic Bullies

Another area where a great deal of bullying takes place is on university campuses. Several recent surveys have shown that the vast majority of college professors are liberals. Being a liberal is not a problem unless you only teach from a liberal perspective and penalize students with different views. Unfortunately, university professors generally are not held to high standards of fairness by their administrations because the university officers are also liberal.

Case in point: A conservative student at Florida Atlantic University was suspended from school because he refused to participate in a class "exercise." His professor asked the class to write "Jesus" on a piece of paper, place this on the ground, and stomp on it. The student respectfully introduced himself as a devout Mormon, and requested to be excused from the exercise. After the professor insisted, the student went to the professor's superior only to be suspended from school.

What can students and citizens do to fight back against political bias on campus? Fortunately the board of trustees at most institutions of higher learning have a significant number of moderates and conservatives as members. These are frequently people who have had great financial success and have experience in the evenhanded application of rules. Grievances concerning political bias should be brought to these individuals in a formal way and they should not be filtered through a university official. Electronic, print, and social media should also be used to publicize the state of affairs if efficient action is not taken by the board of trustees. Most universities are terrified of substantiated negative information about their practices and will act if grievances are brought in a responsible way to their attention. Inaction by the grieved parties will only guarantee continuance of the grievance.

Bullies in Business

Business entities such as stores and organizations that sell products are especially vulnerable to publicized accusations of bullying and unfairness. Their public persona is their most valuable asset and they can ill afford boycotts or public demonstrations against them. For example, a few years ago a large big-box store chain banned its employees from saying "Merry Christmas." The negative press associated with this was so significant that they relented the following Christmas season, an excellent lesson for other retailers.

One of the best examples in American history of collective community action to change grossly unfair practices was the Montgomery bus boycott in the 1950s. The most powerless members of the community, namely the blacks, were able to bring the racist business community to its knees by effectively withholding financial resources, which are the lifeblood of any business. If it is difficult to rally support against what you feel is an unjust practice, it might be wise to reexamine the situation and get other opinions to determine whether you are justified in your opinion.

Unintentional Bullying

Sometimes bullying is not blatant or even intentional. In 2004 my colleagues and I took on the case of the Block conjoined twins from Germany. They were type 1 vertical craniopagus, which means they were joined at the top of the head facing in the same direction. By this time I had learned a great deal about conjoined twins and decided on a new approach. Since the neurosurgical department at Johns Hopkins is rated number one in the country and because I had so many incredibly talented colleagues, I felt it would be wise to involve as many of them as possible in the attempted separation. Some people were renowned vascular neurosurgeons, while others specialized in tumors and tissue separation and others were very skilled with osseous endeavors. By slotting each team into the operation when we reached the part where their expertise would be most valuable, we were able to proceed rapidly with the separation and in fact were ten hours ahead of schedule when the heart of one of the twins (who had had multiple cardiac problems during anesthetic procedures prior to the operation) stopped.

Fortunately CPR was successful, but I knew we had to do more to take care of the problem. I was quite concerned about the heart problems of the one twin and suggested that we consider placing a temporary pacemaker before continuing the operation in a couple of days. One of the anesthesiologists involved was quite adamant that we did not need a pacemaker and that that was his area of expertise. The pediatric cardiologists had mixed views about what should be done. Eventually we proceeded with the rest of the separation without a pacemaker. Unfortunately, at the conclusion of the operation the twin with a weak heart once again suffered a cardiac arrest but this time could not be revived. Fortunately the other twin did well, but we were all quite devastated by the loss of our patient.

In this case I felt quite strongly that a pacemaker should have been placed and that it would have given us a better chance of avoiding tragedy. Afterward I realized that I had too easily yielded to someone who claimed to be a greater authority on the issue. I clearly should have pushed harder for my point of view since the benefit-to-risk ratio would have been favorable for pacemaker versus no pacemaker. By the same token, in situations outside the operating room it is valuable to look at the benefit-to-risk ratio to determine how hard to fight. Of course one needs to be well informed on the issues before making such an analysis, but the rewards can be substantial.

People are unintentionally bullied all the time by political correctness, which keeps them from saying what they really want to say, because they feel that they will be ostracized and disliked. Everyone likes to feel as though they are a part of the community and appreciated, and that makes them relatively easy to bully into compliance and/or silence. Instead of succumbing to bullies, Americans need to grow backbones, examine their understanding of an issue, and push back if they are sure they are right. Being temporarily unpopular for your political view is a small price to pay for moving our nation back from the brink of disaster.

Our Heritage of Courage

The American colonialists were quite content with British oversight until that oversight became burdensome with ever-increasing taxes and abuse of power. If the British government's thirst for the resources of the colonialists had not grown so large, Americans might never have sought independence, but it is the natural tendency of all governments to grow, and they require revenue to do so. Fortunately for America, the rebellion against the English crown was successful and a new era of freedom sprang up on this continent.

The same thing is happening in America today that happened to the colonialists of old. As our government grows larger and more complex, it will require increasingly larger proportions of the people's earnings. Also, as the rights of the government increase, the rights of the people decrease. The question is will the American people of today be as courageous and tough as the colonialists were and are they ready for the ultimate push back? Are they ready to stand boldly for those things they believe in without fear of consequences and are they willing to fight with all tools available to them against those who wish to change the nature of the country from people-centric to government-centric?

Dire Consequences of Giving In

Throughout history many societies have failed to push back and have allowed an overly aggressive government to expand and dominate their lives. Nazi Germany is a perfect example of such a society. One can only wonder what would've happened if people had not tolerated the foolishness of Adolf Hitler's appeal to the baser instincts of greed and envy and his institution of an official weapons confiscation program. He made one group of Germans feel that the success of another group was impeding their own financial progress. He trumped up reasons to confiscate the populace's weapons to quell any subsequent ideas about resistance. His regime may have started out innocently enough, but because the people did not oppose a progressively overreaching government, the entire world suffered a great Holocaust. Some may say that I'm being overly dramatic in comparing U.S. circumstances with Germany's state of affairs before pure evil gained the upper hand there, but few people have recognized the precursors of national societal tragedies and even fewer have done anything about them. Bullies do whatever they can get away with and keep pushing the boundaries until they meet resistance. It is the people's job to stop them before they become uncontrollable.

Push Back Peacefully and Consistently

Lest anyone get the wrong impression, I am not advocating armed insurrection, but rather just making ourselves aware of what is going on vis-à-vis our freedom. It is ineffective to sit around and complain while the encroachment continues. Instead, concerned citizens should be educating their neighbors, circulating petitions, having community discussions that involve their elected representatives, and using social media to get others involved in the struggle to return power to the people and reduce government's size and influence. Every activist has a sphere of influence and at the very least can inform friends about voting issues.

Fighting back against bullies does not always result in immediate victory and, in some cases, you will be soundly defeated. However, bullies like soft targets and if you continue to fight every time they infringe on your rights, you will eventually wear them down and they will look for easier targets. Bullies are cowards, and they will not pick on those who fight back for long.

Win Through Respect

Standing up to bullies doesn't always mean fighting them directly. As I mentioned at the beginning of the chapter, there is another option: gaining their respect. One of the best examples of this kind of pushing back is about a young female substitute teacher at my high school in Detroit. Substitute teachers were often treated quite roughly, but this teacher, who was very short in stature, commanded classrooms where you could hear a pin drop because even the biggest and toughest guys were afraid of her. She was not a mean person, but she consistently refused to tolerate disrespect and insubordination. She was very warm toward students who behaved themselves. One might say she became the bully, but in fact, she was just taking a strong, principled stand that demanded respect, while at the same time being respectful of others.

In fighting back against the secular progressives who wish to control our lives with big government, it is important not to emulate their behavior with respect to denigrating their enemies with name-calling and lies. Instead, be calm and courteous and even nice, because as the Bible says in Proverbs 25:21-22, "If your enemies are hungry, give them food to eat. If they are thirsty, give them water to drink. You will heap burning coals on their heads, and the Lord will reward you." In other words, your enemy will feel much worse if you treat him nicely than if you retaliate. This does not mean that you shouldn't expose what your enemies are doing and that you shouldn't have a plan of counterattack that is wise and well thought out.

Know Your Enemy

A final word on bullies: It is very important to know who your "enemies" are. They are not your average fellow Americans. Don't mistake neighbors who simply disagree with you for bullies—they are your teammates who happen to have different points of view. Disagree with them, try to educate them, learn from them yourself, but don't fight them. Instead, push back against the real bullies—those people and influences that wish to fundamentally change America to another type of society. They can belong to any political party and frequently they disguise themselves as great humanitarians. Unless you understand the philosophy of freedom that created our nation and carefully compare new ideas and actions against that philosophy, it becomes very difficult to determine who and what forces are trying to change the nature of our country. Keen observation of current events and diligent study of history and current events is the best way to determine who the enemies of the American Dream are. Once you identify these bullies, you can stand up to them with courage, and they will back down.

Action Steps

1. Devise a rational plan to confront a bully in your life.
2. Discuss responses to bullying with young people in your sphere of influence.
3. Examine your own behavior for bullying. If any behavior could come even close to being considered bullying, determine to stop the behavior for a month and see whether your life improves.
4. Based on this chapter, try to identify some media and/ or political bullies and discuss your findings with others.

RESPECTFUL DISAGREEMENT

So discuss the matter with them [your neighbors] privately.
Don't tell anyone else, or others may accuse you of gossip.
Then you will never regain your good reputation.

PROVERBS 25:9-10

Recently I had an opportunity to seek funding for the Carson Scholars Fund from a very large and well-funded foundation. I explained that the purpose of the fund is to honor students from all backgrounds who achieve at the highest academic levels and also care about others, placing them on the same kind of pedestal upon which we place athletic superstars. By receiving recognition, money, a medal, the trophy, and an opportunity to attend an awards ceremony, the students frequently rise from nerd to symbol of excellence in the eyes of their peers, and they inspire other students to work toward academic and humanitarian excellence. The other part of the program concentrates on placing reading rooms all over the country to encourage the love of reading. Special emphasis is placed on Title I schools, where many students come from homes with no books and attend schools with no libraries and are unlikely to otherwise establish a love of reading. The extremely elevated high school dropout rate of these schools hurts not only the students but the well-being of the entire country, and we want to help.

I told the foundation staff that their support would allow us to dramatically increase the scope of the program, which is currently active in all fifty states. In response, the staff members were very complimentary about the program and the progress that had been made in a relatively short period of time, but they indicated that their priorities were more global and immediate in nature and would not be able to offer any financial assistance to Carson Scholars.

I feel that the most urgent need in our society is to develop the right kind of leaders for tomorrow, since they will have a tremendous impact not only on the United States but also the world. The foundation staff felt that there were too many problems needing immediate attention and that they could not focus on programs whose effect would be felt in the future. We parted ways cordially and with no hard feelings even though I was disappointed. We both had good intentions but different ideas about priorities. I believe this foundation is composed of good people who expend enormous energy and resources for the good of others and I will continue to have great respect for them regardless of their philosophical priorities.

Though today's politicians would have you think otherwise, it is eminently possible to have substantial disagreements with others and remain friendly and cooperative. This is a lesson that must be quickly relearned by American society if we are to be successful going forward. People will always have different ideas about what is important, but those differences should not trump a cordial working relationship.

Pro-Life versus Pro-Choice

One of the biggest issues dividing Americans today is abortion. Pro-life groups feel that life begins at conception and is very precious and should be protected. They believe that a fetus is a living human being with certain natural rights including life and protection from cruelty. Recent scientific observations have led observers to conclude that a fetus can experience pain as early as ten weeks of gestation. This means that most abortion procedures produce extreme discomfort for the fetus before it dies, making abortion even more abhorrent to pro-life groups. Because of these convictions, some members of pro-life groups oppose abortion under all circumstances, while others believe abortion is wrong but are willing to tolerate abortion in the case of rape, incest, and/ or risk to the mother's life. It is important for the pro-choice groups to understand that the pro-life group is not being mean and obstinate, but truly believes that babies are being slaughtered by people who primarily care about their own convenience.

On the other hand, the pro-life group needs to understand that the pro-choice group does not really believe that the fetus is a real human being entitled to natural human rights. They are not necessarily being mean or selfish, but rather just have a different understanding of when life begins.

This is a difficult issue on which to reach compromise, but that should not mean the members of opposing sides demonize each other. I suspect that over the course of time, the age line for abortions will continue to shift depending on political winds and further scientific information regarding fetal existence. The important thing is for both sides to understand the reasoning that forms the foundation for the beliefs of the other side. It is only through attempted empathy that the two sides can work cordially together.

Welfare

Another contentious issue is whether welfare should be extended to able-bodied adults. In recent years the welfare rolls have rapidly expanded, dramatically adding to the national debt. Those who are in favor of welfare reform tend to claim that people on welfare are lazy and that those who want to continue supporting them are wasteful spendthrifts. Those on the other side tend to call their opponents hard-hearted skinflints who do not care about the poor. The reality is that none of this name-calling is necessary.

If those on each side of the issue would try to place themselves in the shoes of those with whom they disagree, much of the rancor would dissolve. If you suddenly fell on hard times, it is very likely that you would welcome public assistance, even for an extended period. If, as is true in many cases, you could live better on the welfare system than you could working a low-wage job, what would you do? Certainly if one has small children to care for, elderly parents, or a sick family member, it would make a lot more sense to stay home and accept the public assistance than to try to work. I certainly would not criticize someone who has made such a decision under these circumstances, and it is important for those who are not on public assistance to understand this kind of reasoning.

On the other hand, if you had been on public assistance for a while and suddenly got off it because you got a low-paying job (or more than one to make ends meet), you probably wouldn't be overly excited about being forced to support those who are less fortunate. If you are making a good salary, you may be happy to share with the less fortunate, or you might feel taken advantage of by a system that requires more of your resources to support ever-expanding government entitlements. Those on welfare should make an attempt to understand how these people feel as well.

Doctors Versus Patients

Another example of an issue on which we can respectfully disagree and still work together is tort reform. One of the real drivers of medical costs is the practice of defensive medicine. Many lawyers are happy to bring a lawsuit against a doctor or his practice knowing that they will receive 30 to 40 percent of the award. Eighty to 90 percent of neurosurgical malpractice cases are without merit but that matters little to these lawyers because the majority of cases are settled, since the doctor, the hospital, and the insurance company are not interested in being tied up in a court case for several months. Once the monetary demand drops to an acceptable level, they would rather pay the settlement and move on.

In order to protect themselves from lawsuits, many doctors order a lot of unnecessary tests and screenings so they can't be accused of negligence, driving health care costs up. Doctors also purchase extremely expensive insurance to guard themselves against lawsuits, which further inflates what they charge

patients. Worst of all, some of the best doctors have quit prac-
ticing after enduring unjustified lawsuits, further impoverishing
our already broken health care system.

Those against tort reform argue that we need the lawsuits in
order to police the medical industry. They feel that unscrupu-
lous medical professionals would treat patients poorly without
the threat of a lawsuit over their heads. Those on the other side
of the argument would say that in countries where there is no
medical malpractice crisis, the doctors have not abandoned
common decency and caring about their patients. Both are reasonable positions, and if the opposing sides would disagree respectfully, they might be able to pass reform similar to that
passed in California, which halted a substantial exodus of physicians from the state. Instead, every time tort reform has been
introduced to Congress, certain senators have filibustered the
issue to death instead of discussing the issue reasonably.

The Rich Versus the Poor

One of the biggest bones of contention in our nation revolves
around the definition of fair taxation. According to some, fair
taxation means taking progressively more from the rich and
redistributing it to others after the government takes its "fair
share." Others argue that we should reward the wealthy with
tax breaks, trusting that the wealth will "trickle down." I believe there is a third way that becomes evident once you consider the viewpoints of both the rich and the poor.

I think if a poor person puts herself into the shoes of a rich
person, she would feel largely responsible for the well-being of
society because her profitable lifestyle has resulted in signifi-

cant income to sustain the rest of society. If a rich person were put into the shoes of a poor person, he would likely already have a significantly developed work ethic and rather than complaining about having to contribute anything from his meager salary toward societal maintenance, he would be thinking about how to enhance his income and his life. Both would realize that the rich and the poor all have rights and responsibilities in society.

Considering the views of both the rich and the poor, I would argue that fair taxation means that everyone contributes according to their ability, or in other words, proportionately. I like the idea of proportionality because that was put forth in the Bible in the concept of tithing. All taxpayers were required to give 10 percent of their increase. If they had no increase they had to give nothing, and if they had an extralarge increase, they still only had to provide 10 percent of their increase. This system recognized that the wealthy were not above the law—no tax breaks and no political clout for having given a larger amount. It also recognized that the poor were not "below" the law—as dignified human beings, they had responsibilities to give, even if just a little.

If our society used this system, a Wall Street mogul who made $10 billion would be required to give $1 billion and a Harlem schoolteacher who made $50,000 would be required to give $5,000. Even though one would give hundreds of times more than the other, they would both have one vote and the same rights and responsibilities before our government. This fits with the American idea that everybody contributes to the overall good of society with the talents he or she brings to the table, no matter how much money each has. Schoolteachers offer much in terms of training the next generation, whereas billionaires offer much in terms of providing resources to maintain infrastructure and so on that benefit everyone.

Not everyone agrees with this plan. Some feel that it is fair for those with incomes under a certain dollar amount not to pay any federal tax. They say that these people are too poor and it would be a great burden to require them to contribute to the common pot. While I appreciate their compassion, serious problems arise when a person who pays nothing has the right to vote and determine what other people are paying. It does not make sense for me to vote on how much you should give if I don't have to give anything. In fact, in such a situation it is likely that I would be more than willing to vote to raise your taxes while I simply reap the benefits.

Unfortunately, redistributionism is a very good strategy for cultivating the favor of large blocks of voters. Under this system, voters will always be loyal to that politician who promises to keep taxes low or nonexistent while taking from the "evil rich" to support the government. Voters with lower incomes will always have the incentive to vote for higher taxes on the wealthy, and that system would result in a smaller and smaller tax base supporting an increasingly large financial burden.

As soon as you introduce a graduated income tax as opposed to a proportional income tax, you also introduce your own biases. Although it sounds magnanimous to say the rich should bear virtually all of the tax burden and the poor should not have their lives complicated by paying any taxes, this is actually quite demeaning to the poor and is basically saying to them, "You poor little thing, don't you worry because I will take care of you since you can't take care of yourself." Robbing people of dignity by making them feel like freeloaders is not compassionate, but it can be quite effective in assuaging the guilt of some of the economically well-off individuals in our society.

Not only is this kind of taxation both divisive and unsustainable, it is especially offensive to individuals like me who have worked extremely hard throughout life to achieve success and who give away enormous amounts of money to benefit others. This system unfairly assumes that people like me are only greedy and uncaring. Wealthy people in the United States have created more charitable organizations and been more philanthropic than any other group in the world. We should celebrate their achievements rather than envy them.

Sure, some wealthy people are selfish because they are human beings subject to the same imperfections as everyone else. Fortunately, even these people have to give back to society; they need house cleaners, pilots, gardeners, chauffeurs, cooks, and a host of other people to maintain their lifestyle. Even if they don't have a charitable bone in their body, they still provide employment for others. We are more likely to get such individuals to begin thinking of others if we treat them fairly rather than if we demonize them, just as the poor are more likely to want compromise if we don't assume they are all lazy and undeserving of help.

The Importance of Humility and a Listening Ear

There are many more contentious issues that divide the American people, but all of them should be subjected to open civil discussions in which each side tries to look at the issue from the perspective of the other. This can only be done if each party is willing to exhibit some humility. That means being willing to let someone else be right sometimes and being willing to listen.

I was recently on a national talk show in which I represented one side of a particular argument and a congresswoman represented the other side. She was so intent on demonstrating the superiority of her position that she repeatedly rudely interrupted while I was speaking without even realizing that we were largely in agreement. I can certainly identify with this attitude, because I held an extreme version of it as an adolescent in Detroit. I arrogantly thought that I knew more than others and I frequently would not even entertain their views. I often found myself in trouble, because I would become angry and react in a violent or other aggressive manner, in one case almost killing a classmate with a knife.

I had been minding my own business when a classmate came along and began to ridicule me. I had a large camping knife in my hand and without thinking, I lunged at him, plunging the knife into his abdomen. He backed off, certain that he had been mortally wounded before discovering that the knife blade had struck a large metal belt buckle under his clothing and broken. He fled in terror but I was even more terrified when realizing that I had almost killed someone. That incident led me to prayerfully consider my plight and to ask for God's guidance and help. I came to understand that very day that I was always angry because I was selfish. I felt that someone was always infringing on my rights, getting in my space, messing with my things, disregarding my positions, and so on, which offended me, leading to inappropriate behavior. Through wisdom provided by God it dawned on me that I should step outside of the center of the circle so that everything wasn't always about me. I learned to consider the viewpoint of others and it dramatically altered my behavior. Most people who know me today cannot believe that I was ever plagued by a violent temper. Proverbs 16:32 says, "It is better to be patient than powerful; it is better to have self-control than to conquer a city." Anyone can act irrationally, but it takes a wise and truly strong individual to remain controlled, logical, and willing to truly hear what the other person is saying.

Strategies for Cordial Disagreement

Compromise is most likely when both parties respect each other no matter how much they disagree. In stressful situations where you need a consensus, respect sometimes means saying nothing and refraining from name-calling even when irritated. By doing so, you not only manifest respect for others but for yourself as well. The best way to respond to distracting personal attacks is to practice bringing the conversation back to the issue at hand. Never fall into the trap of engaging in personal attacks while letting the topic of conversation slip into the background. Doing so allows your opponent to escape the need to explain her position. If she has a good argument, she would be eager to pursue it rather than trying to change the subject to you and your character.

When seeking respectful dialogue, another good tactic is to focus on the big picture and de-emphasize small details. I liken the silly arguments that some people engage in to a passenger ship that is about to go over Niagara Falls while the passengers and crew are arguing about the barnacles on the side of the ship. They continue a discourse that could have some value down the road, but they fail to adjust the course of the ship and everyone perishes, rendering the barnacle issue completely irrelevant. Don't lose sight of the issue at hand.

I have found that the best way to proceed with civil discussions about issues on which people disagree is to first concur on what is important to both parties. Next determine who is harmed by each position and agree not to intentionally harm others. Last, exhibit tolerance without discarding core values.

The Second Amendment debate is a good illustration of this process. Some people feel that there should be no restrictions on the rights of citizens to have any kind of weapon they choose. They firmly believe that the Second Amendment was established to allow citizens to protect themselves from foreign or domestic threats including an out-of-control central government. They do not believe it reasonable for such a government to hold all of the powerful weapons, while they are left with only hunting rifles.

The other side dismisses such arguments as paranoia and believes in stringent gun control and restrictions on the types of weapons and amount of ammunition individuals can possess. They believe that we could quell the epidemic of mass murders by keeping dangerous weapons out of the hands of unstable individuals.

Both sides can agree that we do not want dangerous weapons in the hands of unstable individuals and this should be the starting point of any conversation. The first group would probably agree that freedom is the most important thing, while the second group might feel that safety is the most important thing. Their discussion should center around how to preserve Second Amendment freedom while ensuring safety for the largest number of citizens. During those discussions both should agree to hold personal freedom and societal safety as their targets. Nothing should be done to intentionally affect those two things in a negative way. This is a civilized way to have a productive discussion and is the first step toward finding compromise.

Recall that I love to say, "If two people agree about everything, one of them isn't necessary." Disagreement is part of being a person who has choices. One of those choices is to respect others and engage in intelligent conversation about differences of opinion without becoming enemies, eventually allowing us to move forward to compromise. "A house divided against itself cannot stand," and a nation that tears itself apart will not survive.

Action Steps

1. Take the first step and offer to put your differences aside with someone you frequently argue with. Refuse to argue with them for at least one month.
2. If engaged in a pointless argument, change the subject to something about which there is agreement.
3. Try to conceive of a plan that might work for both sides when you see the next political argument on television.
4. Try listening twice as much as talking since you have two ears and only one mouth.

10

THE ART OF COMPROMISE

Without wise leadership, a nation falls; with many counselors,
there is safety.

PROVERBS 11:14

Although we had very little money, my mother would save every penny over several years in order to be able to purchase a
new car when the old one she was driving was on its last leg. She
did not believe in buying used cars, because she felt that the
previous owner probably would not have gotten rid of it if it was
functioning optimally.

Once when I was a teenager I went with her to look at a car.
It was a beautiful vehicle, yellow with black interior and a black
vinyl top. I was quite excited, because I had recently acquired
my driver's license and was already starting to imagine myself
cruising down the streets of Detroit in a brand-new automobile.
The problem was that the car was several hundred dollars more
expensive than the cash she had on hand.

My mother could bargain with the best of people, and after
a couple of hours had worn the salesman down to the point

that he was ready to make a deal after she showed him the cash. I was absolutely jubilant until I heard several days later that the salesman had lost his job for giving my mother too sweet a deal. I'm certain that if my mother had had more money, she would have been willing to compromise, but she believed in only paying cash for cars and would not qualify for a loan anyway. As a matter of principle, she did not believe in borrowing money to pay for anything other than a house, because she had seen too many people ruin their lives with financial overreach.

Many people feel that driving a hard bargain is a sign of strength and perseverance, and in many cases they are correct. However, my mother and I learned the hard way that it is not always the kindest thing to do. My mother certainly did not intend to get the man fired and offered to give the car back, but for some reason, since the deal had already been consummated, that was not possible. While my mother was pleased she had been able to buy the car, she wished she had not pressed so hard. Sometimes compromise is the best way to go, even when you think you could get your own way without it.

Many people have recently commented on how difficult it is to get anything accomplished in Washington anymore. The art of compromise appears to be vanishing with both political parties adopting a "my way or the highway" attitude. In much of the legislation that has been passed in the last few years, one side is pleased and the other side is disgruntled. This is an acceptable outcome, as long as each side is civil and works honestly with the other. Unfortunately today, both parties seem to be content with gridlock if they can't get what they want and have stopped giving ground in order to be a part of an important solution. Rather than sulking, they should be seeking compromise in every possible way. For that to happen, both sides must have some incentive to move through respectful disagreement to produce an actual agreement.

Timing Is Everything

I remember as a child in Boston going to Haymarket Square on Saturday evenings with my mother and my aunt and uncle, as well as my brother. This was the weekly trip to buy produce and I always found it exciting, especially during the closing hour when the farmers were ready to go home and wanted desperately to avoid carrying unsold produce back home. The same sellers who a couple of hours earlier were disinclined to sell five tomatoes for a dollar were now willing to give away a dozen tomatoes for the same price. You might say they were highly incentivized to make a deal.

In the same way, situations change for legislators and it is good to revisit issues periodically where no compromise was possible earlier. A good example of this is the fierce opposition to Medicare when it was first introduced. While some lawmakers refused it initially, it soon became apparent that there were no other good alternatives being offered, and the need for the program grew as our population began showing significant signs of aging. Over time, the incentive for compromising grew, the opposition waned, and the program was accepted by both legislative bodies.

Starting Small

When I was a freshman in high school, my Latin class had to break up into teams and complete a complex project depicting some important facet of the Roman Empire. I was paired with a couple of people who had always been my academic competitors and with whom I did not get along particularly well. Despite our dislike for one another, we got to work and decided to create a replica of the Roman Colosseum. We experimented with all types of ingredients and finally decided to construct walls with dough, clay, and sand. We used wire and popsicle sticks for scaffolding, and really tested our artistic talents in the creation of people and ferocious animals to populate a structure that was rather magnificent, if I do say so myself. In the process of doing the research and figuring out how to make our project structurally sound and aesthetically pleasing, we began to realize that we liked one another and started to associate as friends as much as project mates.

I believe the same thing could happen in Washington with our legislators if they put aside their differences and worked together in a systematic fashion to solve a problem. Perhaps they could start with a small issue and work their way up gradually to large and very meaningful problems. I believe they would discover in working together that they are not nearly as different from one another as they had previously thought.

Recent Examples of Compromise

Interestingly enough, there already have been a number of such projects, and the records are available for our study. We have the opportunity to see what kind of people have been representing us, and whether they are interested in serving the needs of the populace or whether they are more closely tied to the special interest groups that continue to fund their reelection. We have all the ammunition we need to make important decisions about our nation's direction.

In our recent history, there have been some notable events that brought both parties together with an amazing show of unity and success. The Iraqi invasion of Kuwait led to a bipartisan determination to expel Saddam Hussein and his army from the land of the peace-loving people of Kuwait. Even more unity was demonstrated after our nation was attacked by radical Islamic elements on September 11, 2001. People were able to look at the big picture in these situations and quickly establish common goals that were reached through cooperative efforts. In the latter case a second war ensued that probably was not necessary, but there was bipartisan agreement on its initiation, although bitter partisan battles over the war effort later broke out.

During the Clinton administration there was significant rancor between the two parties over efforts to reform social welfare programs. Both sides made significant concessions and successfully improved the program while decreasing the welfare rolls. At the beginning of the welfare fight, both sides were entrenched and it appeared that no progress would be made, but President Clinton exercised real leadership by sitting down with Speaker Gingrich and discussing how to make changes that would make the program affordable while still helping those individuals who were truly in need. These kinds of cooperative efforts actually led to a budgetary surplus for the first time in many years. There is absolutely no reason why the same type of success cannot be achieved today if the two sides were willing to look at the big picture and put aside pride in order to solve problems, with no one achieving total victory and no one suffering total defeat.

Gay Marriage

One large issue that is ripe for compromise is the issue of gay marriage. I liken the gay marriage argument to a new group of mathematicians who claim that $2 + 2 = 5$. The traditional mathematicians say that $2 + 2 = 4$ and always has been, and always will be 4. The new mathematicians continue to insist on their version of mathematics so the traditional mathematicians eventually relent and say, "For you guys, $2 + 2 = 5$, but for us it will continue to be 4." The new mathematicians are not satisfied with that compromise and say that $2 + 2$ must also be 5 for you and everyone else and if you won't accept that then you are a "mathist" (as opposed to a racist, sexist, or some other kind of "ist") or mathophobe. The two sides will most likely never reach an agreement as to the actual equation. If, however, they discuss the matter rationally without demanding that political correctness silence the other's opinions, they may move through respectful disagreement to practical compromises that are acceptable to both sides.

I firmly believe that marriage is between a man and a woman. However, I see no reason why any two consenting adults, regardless of their sexual orientation, cannot be joined together in a legally binding civil relationship that provides hospital visitation rights, property rights, and so on without tampering with the definition of marriage. This would give the gay population what they want, while leaving the traditional definition of marriage intact. This is what compromise is about. The "my way or the highway" mentality on either side of the argument only leads to gridlock and animosity. This is a practical way to apply common sense to a complex social issue.

National Debt

Another issue where compromise is badly needed is rapidly accumulating debt. The Democrats, led by the president, appear to be relatively unconcerned about the debt and are happy to continue spending, borrowing, and expanding entitlements. The Republicans, on the other hand, are extremely concerned that we will eventually have to pay the piper if we continue to expand our national debt, and that we will burden future generations with financial obligations that will extinguish the American Dream. One side is concerned about preserving entitlements and the other is concerned about preserving our nation's future.

A little wisdom and some review of the actual facts would be useful in the pursuit of joint solutions. We have a $17 trillion national debt that continues to grow. We have ever-expanding entitlement programs that are extremely expensive. Small businesses are frightened of government and its plans to implement a health care system that will be expensive and intrusive. This also includes its many enforcement provisions that will be overseen by the discredited IRS, which at the time of this writing is under investigation for illegal activity. Big businesses have trillions of dollars sitting on the sidelines waiting for a friendlier business environment before investing. None of us, regardless of our political philosophy, can possibly be content with such a situation. The injection of a little common sense into the discussions would prove beneficial.

As far as the growing debt is concerned, it should be treated the same way that personal debt is treated by thinking and pragmatic families. First they assess their income and output. If the output is greater than the income, they either decrease the output, find a way to increase the income, or both. If after several months their deficit spending continues, they realize that their plan is not working and honestly reappraise and adjust it accordingly. The last thing they do is double down on an ineffective plan while sticking their head in the sand. An unwise family in this situation, however, would continue on, while stating emphatically that they were not spending as much as they had been and that eventually the budget would come under control. They would claim that it would be too painful to significantly cut down on the spending and that anyone requesting such action is obviously heartless. They would also talk about growing their income, but would not change what they were doing to make that a reality. When they saw that things were not working out according to their predictions, they would never consider that they were following an inappropriate course of action, but instead would blame others for impeding them.

There's no question that our government needs to cut wasteful spending. Obviously the cutting should occur in areas of duplication of services, extravagant entertainment for government officials, fraud, unnecessary programs, and so on. In the recent sequestration efforts, the current administration intentionally targeted cuts that would be felt acutely by the public who would then agree that making any cuts was too painful.

Included in these cuts was elimination of White House tours for ordinary citizens. This is something that many school groups plan for years and it is not too expensive. Additionally, in light of this particular cut, many individuals and groups volunteered to provide the funds necessary to keep the White House tours open, but such offers were refused. Another cut was in TSA (Transportation Security Administration) personnel to make the experience at the airport even more painful for travelers. I personally find these tactics extraordinarily insulting to the populace's intelligence, most of whom can easily see through this gamesmanship. The sad thing is that there are large numbers of people in American society today who are fooled by these infantile tactics and don't question anything, as long as they get their government support.

Much more important, however, than cutting money from the budget, is expanding the economy with resultant significant income to the government. We do not have to reinvent the wheel to accomplish this. We simply need to create a friendly environment for business and entrepreneurship and stop trying to regulate the lives of responsible American citizens. These were principles that were followed (early in American history) during the rapid expansion of business and industry throughout our nation, which rapidly propelled us to the pinnacle of the world economically.

First of all, we need to recognize that the United States has the highest corporate tax rates in the world. Our rates even exceed those of openly socialist countries. A few years ago Canada and several other countries significantly slashed their corporate rates, which had the desired effect of attracting American business. Our American leadership has talked about cutting corporate tax rates, but nothing has been done. We are capable of moving very quickly in a crisis, such as 9/11, but extreme lethargy characterizes our usual pace of governmental progress. This is an issue that should not be controversial for those who are socialists in our Congress.

More controversial, however, is the issue of cutting tax rates for individuals and small businesses. The Democrats feel that those with very high incomes should pay most of the taxes since they can afford to do so. The Republicans feel that enabling people to keep the vast majority of what they earn is more conducive to growth and encourages people to work hard. Again, a little common sense goes a long way. Taxation needs to be fair for everyone and not just for a favored group. This is the reason I like the tithing model set forth in the Bible, as I mentioned earlier. As soon as you depart from a proportional taxation system, you introduce ideological bias, making arguments endless. Also, everyone must have skin in the game when it comes to taxation. People with a lot of money have a large amount of skin in the game and people with very little money only have a small amount, but everybody is taxed proportionately, which makes it fair.

Unfairness is introduced when the tax code is riddled with loopholes that are accessible to some but irrelevant for others. Those with good tax lawyers and accountants can substantially reduce the taxes they pay, which is grossly unfair to those unable to take advantage of such things. Lowering tax rates and eliminating loopholes at the same time is a no-brainer that has been advocated by both Republicans and Democrats, but once again nothing is done. Even with the loopholes, the top 10 percent of the populace in terms of income pay 70 percent of the income taxes while earning 46 percent of the taxable income, which means they are indeed paying more than their fair share.

The Simpson-Bowles commission, which was a bipartisan congressional group, laid out the rationale for cutting taxes and eliminating loopholes quite cogently and in a way that provided a victory for both sides, but the recommendations were rejected by the executive branch of government and by members of Congress from both sides. This is a good example of the "my way or the highway" philosophy that runs rampant in Washington today. Ideology generally does not yield to logic and common sense. Because the Simpson-Bowles plan and other plans like it significantly reduced government spending and thus government growth, those politicians who feel that government is the solution to every problem and want to massively expand the government's reach into every aspect of our lives could not possibly agree with a reasoned approach to getting our deficit under control and growing the economy. At the same time, those who want to rapidly reduce the federal debt and shrink government might be noble in their goals, but must be patient and gradually accomplish their objectives, because a rapid reduction in the size of government could create significant unemployment and other logistical problems that could be avoided with some compromise.

The Problem of Pride

In the Bible, in the Book of Proverbs we are told that God hates pride and arrogance. These are the very characteristics that surround the ideologues on both sides who feel that their way is the only right way. How many wonderful relationships never developed because each of the two parties was too proud to make the first move? How many wonderful marriages were ruined because pride erased the words "I'm sorry" from a couple's vocabularies? I vividly remember a case where a couple lost their home to foreclosure because they refused to accept a bid from a buyer that was lower than their asking price. Pride is the quickest compromise killer.

When this kind of silliness is not only present but abounds in our congressional and executive halls, how can we ever expect to make progress? The answer to this problem is simple. It is found in the Bible, again in the Book of Proverbs where chapter 22, verse 4 says, "True humility and fear of the Lord lead to riches, honor, and long life." Humility doesn't mean that you can't have an opinion or advocate a position, but it does mean you are willing to consider the opinions and positions of others in a serious way and then move forward to a meaningful compromise. If the politicians can just drop some of the hubris and once again serve humbly for the good of the people, solutions will rapidly follow. We the people must make ourselves aware of whom the politicians are who totally disregard our welfare and cast their votes in their own interests. Those people need to be thrown out of office on a wholesale basis regardless of their party affiliation.

Action Steps

1. Try to identify some national politicians who are humble.
2. Identify your principles that can't be compromised. Then

consider what ideas used to implement those principles could be compromised.

3. Make the first step toward compromise of an idea that has put you at odds with someone you know.

4. Examine your own attitude for arrogance. When you identify an area of pride, practice gratitude for what you have been given. Recognize your own fallibility.

BECOMING INFORMED

> Only simpletons believe everything they are told! The prudent carefully consider their steps.
>
> PROVERBS 14:15

When I was young, I thought classical music was only the background noise for cartoons, so when my brother Curtis returned from one of his stints in the navy with an album titled *The Unfinished Symphony of Franz Schubert*, I was quite astonished. This was a strange choice for someone who had grown up in Detroit, also known as Motown. In Detroit "classical" music was produced by the likes of Stevie Wonder, the Supremes, the Temptations, the Four Tops, Gladys Knight, Martha and the Vandellas, and the Jackson Five.

Nevertheless, I listened to the Unfinished Symphony, and it appealed to me. I was interested in learning more about classical music because they frequently asked questions on my favorite television program, *GE College Bowl,* about different classical composers and their creations. Inspired by Curtis, I purchased a record album of Rossini overtures that included the theme from the *Lone Ranger*. I played that record every day until I could name each overture and became immensely fond of this music, which led me to begin listening to classical music stations and making classical music a big part of my life. I'm glad I cultivated the interest, since classical music affected my life in many ways and, most important, created some wonderful friendships, including a lasting relationship with a young Yale student by the name of Candy Rustin, a classical violinist who is now my wife of thirty-eight years.

Many people criticized me and thought that I was weird because of my love of classical music, but if I had listened to them and remained in the ideological box they created for themselves, I would not have expanded my horizons in a way that turned out to be positive for me. Today I frequently find myself reminding young people to expand their horizons of knowledge and not listen to those who tell them to limit their interests to things that are "culturally relevant." I tell them that if you want to be relevant only in your household, then you only need to know the things that are important in your house, and if you want to be relevant in your neighborhood, you need to know what's important in your neighborhood. The same thing applies to your city, state, and country. And if you want to be relevant to the entire world, program that computer known as your brain with all kinds of information from everywhere in order to prepare yourself.

Someone might say, "Don't learn all that stuff because you will overload your brain." As a neuroscientist I can tell you unequivocally that it is impossible to overload the human brain with information. If you learn one new fact every second, which is virtually impossible, it will take you approximately three million years to approach brain overload. The human brain has billions of neurons and hundreds of billions of interconnections. It can process more than two million bits of information per second and can remember everything you have ever seen or heard.

All of this information is retained indefinitely. I could take an eighty-five-year-old man and place depth electrodes into a certain part of his brain followed by appropriate electrical stimulation and he would be able to recite back verbatim a book he had read sixty years ago. Most of us can't retrieve the information our brain stores that easily, but surely we can improve.

Many people comment on what percentage of the brain we actually use, but no one knows the actual number. We do, however, know of many accounts of individuals who have done unbelievable things when it was a matter of survival. That alone tells us that we generally operate significantly below capacity and that we can always learn more.

Education as the Foundation of Our Government

The founders of our nation understood that such a society could not long exist without a well-informed and well-educated populace who used the amazing brains God gave them. Even people with only a grade school education in America in the 1800s were extremely well educated. That education in turn allowed them to make informed decisions in the voting booth, protecting them against tyranny.

There are many sinister forces that are vying for power in

our American society. Most of these are associated with politically ambitious individuals who are far more concerned about power and prestige than they are about the people's welfare. Uninformed citizens tend to be trusting of some of these forces without doing due diligence in terms of studying their previous performance or their associations with dubious characters. An uninformed voter, for instance, might ignore the fact that their favorite candidate had a long history of associating with radical elements, because the candidate proclaims his good intentions and promises them justice. A well-informed voter who favored the same candidate might engage in further investigation on his own, discover that the candidate represented an organization found to be engaged in illegal practices, and change his vote as a result of the discovery.

Congress today has less than a 10 percent approval rating, yet its members are reelected 90 percent of the time across the nation. This means they have been successful in fooling the voters, but it does not mean that this should or will continue. Until the laws of this country are changed, we the people still have the ability to select our representatives. This is not only a right, but a responsibility, and we can only exercise that right responsibly when we are well informed.

Know the Record, Not Just the Party

To be informed voters, Americans need to learn to look beyond party affiliation. A significant number of voters enter the voting booth looking for a name they recognize or a party affiliation and they cast their vote based on these superficial factors. Honest politicians should be uncomfortable cultivating these types of voters. Dishonest politicians actively try to encourage such voters to support them by offering promises of jobs, free or low-cost health care, easy access to citizenship for aliens, free equipment such as telephones, and government aid to purchase food and other necessities. These bribes are extraordinarily appealing to people who feel disempowered, yet entitled. The politicians know that all of these promises will not be fulfilled or will only be fulfilled temporarily before money runs out, but they don't really care as long as they are voted into power. The poor voters in many cases are too stressed to even notice the poor performance of their representatives and eagerly listen while those same representatives shower them with even more empty promises.

Unfortunately, many Americans don't even know who their representatives are, nor are they aware of their voting record or general philosophy about life in our nation. Because the world is so interconnected, a well-informed individual cannot be an isolationist. They clearly must be aware of what is happening in the rest of the world and should be able to articulate opinions on major subjects of interest at any time. This way, they will be able to tell whether their opinions are in sync with those of their state and congressional representatives.

All of this is to say that we as Americans should vigorously pursue knowledge of history, current events, science and technology, finance, geography, philosophy, and religion—actually, anything and everything. Cultivating wide-ranging curiosity and careful study will provide the background we need to correctly analyze the words uttered by politicians and people in the media.

Don't Replace Your Brain with a Computer

I've heard it argued that a broad base of knowledge is not nearly as important as it used to be, because most people have smartphones and can instantly access the Internet. While it may be a waste of time to memorize certain types of information since we all have virtual encyclopedias in our pockets, there is no substitute for an ingrained broad base of knowledge. That built-in knowledge allows a person to immediately assess the veracity of something they are hearing for the first time rather than just swallowing it hook, line, and sinker. While we may be able to look up answers to many questions, the study of psychology has demonstrated that what we already know influences the way we process new information. For instance, if we know there is a rabid dog loose in our neighborhood, we will regard any stray dog with a great deal of caution and suspicion, whereas if we are notified that a valuable prize-winning dog is lost in our neighborhood with a big reward out for its return, we are likely to regard that stray dog differently. Having a good knowledge base rather than relying on the ability to look everything up on Google definitely affects our instant analysis of new information on an everyday basis.

Dangers of Ignorance

Unfortunately, uninformed citizens frequently are the most vociferous in voicing their opinions. They cannot back up those opinions with facts but often are not interested in listening to common sense that opposes their beliefs. I remember a young man, very popular during late middle school and early high school years, who provides a vivid example of this behavior and its consequences. He had a following and clearly was the leader of the pack. He also was quick to voice his opinions about almost everything and was overly impressed with his own physical abilities. One unfortunate summer day, he was bragging about his swimming abilities and when challenged, was determined to demonstrate that his detractors were wrong. On a dare, he attempted to swim to one of the pillars holding up a large bridge and then swim back to shore. Unfortunately, he was caught in the undertow of the river and drowned. His tragic death illustrates what can happen when one pursues goals without appropriate information. One may think that a river looks like a gigantic swimming pool, but a little investigation should lead one to the understanding that there are many forces in a river that are not found in a swimming pool.

While a lack of education can lead to hasty action, it can also lead to lethal inaction. During the last presidential election in America, tens of millions of eligible voters simply did not vote. Many have become frustrated with the whole political scene and do not want to participate, while many others feel that the elections are fixed and/or their vote would not count anyway for a variety of reasons. I cannot emphasize strongly enough to such individuals that your failure to become informed and vote accordingly only exacerbates the situation. If only those completely swayed by the promises of demagogues vote, we will soon be in trouble far deeper than what we have already experienced.

What an Educated Citizen Knows

Becoming an informed citizen not only makes you a wiser voter but can enhance all of life's experiences, from planning a career to raising a family. Time and space won't allow me to provide an exhaustive outline of the things informed citizens should know, but here are a few of the basics:

- Basic world and American history
- Basic world and American geography
- Basic household economics (key principles like balancing a checkbook and knowing that you do not buy a house that costs more than two and a half times your annual income could have spared many Americans a lot of trouble before the housing crisis)
- Basic understanding of how credit works and how debt accumulates
- Names of state and national representatives
- Basic nutrition and disease management
- Traffic rules for pedestrians and vehicle operators
- Basic math including the calculation of percentages
- The ability to read at an eighth-grade level

You may be surprised at the elementary nature of some items on this list, but a surprising number of adult Americans are lacking in these areas despite being well versed in the minor characters of popular sitcoms. Obviously there are a host of other things that would be useful to know, but I've deliberately chosen this list, since anyone who is honest and informed at the basic levels described above will be a formidable individual who is difficult to manipulate and would be a prized supporter for any honest political candidate.

Education Is the Door to Prosperity

It is especially imperative that we emphasize to members of oppressed communities that education affects your entire life. There are many studies available to show vast lifetime economic differences between those with a high school diploma versus a college degree versus a professional degree. (Education in highly skilled trades also pays off very well economically.) The first twenty to twenty-five years are spent either preparing yourself educationally or not preparing yourself. If you prepare well, you will have sixty years to reap the benefits. If you prepare poorly, you will have sixty years to suffer the consequences. When you look at it that way, a little investment in hard work for a relatively short period of time pays huge dividends, while failure to prepare is equivalent to choosing to be a victim of society. We must get our young people to understand that they are the ones who get to make the choice about the lifestyle they will lead. As long as they remain free of legal entanglements, no one can stop them from pursuing their dreams. My life is a testament to this.

Education also opens many doors of personal fulfillment and joy that have nothing to do with economics. I believe it would be highly instructive and beneficial to many of the young people in our nation to live abroad in a third world nation for several months and then return to the United States. Like many immigrants who come here, I believe they would immediately realize how many opportunities they have and how many choices are theirs for the taking.

It's Never Too Late to Learn

The basic elements necessary to become an informed citizen are readily available in the public school systems, but unfortunately some people do not pay attention in school, and 30 percent of those who enter U.S. high schools do not graduate. Fortunately, all hope is not lost for such individuals, because there are many ways that one can acquire the basic knowledge listed in the bullet points above. Information on those topics can be found for free online, though it's important to choose reputable sources. Many things posted on the Internet are simply opinions presented as facts and it is important to cross-reference information several times before accepting them.

Television and radio programs can provide much information on current events, but since there is so much bias in the media, it is important to listen to several sources representing both sides of an issue in order to be informed. Listening only to one cable news outlet is probably not wise if you want to learn about all sides of an issue. The same is true of printed media. I recently had dinner with two senior editors of a major national newspaper and I asked them if they were unbiased. They both proclaimed that they were objective and saw no bias in their reporting, despite clearly partisan leanings in their paper. To avoid absorbing a biased point of view, make sure you vary your media sources.

Perhaps the best source of information are books from reputable publishers. As a boy I made extensive use of the public library, where I could access thousands of books for free. Even such books can give a slanted view, making it wise for the reader to read many books. One way to find out what books are fair and accurate is to ask librarians. In most cases they don't mind being references even if you are not checking out a book from their library. It is also a good idea, when trying to decide how reputable a particular publisher is, to determine the number of books they have in the section of the library that you are interested in. There are numerous small, upstart publishing houses that make claims that cannot be substantiated about the quality of their publications, but if you see their name on numerous titles, it is likely that they are quite reputable and that they engage in due diligence before publishing any work.

Don't Be Fooled

People who try to manipulate public opinion are much more effective when they appear to present new information to people who should have already known the subject matter. They also like to make accusations against their enemies, repeating them loudly and often with the hope that people will begin to believe them. They know that even though they frequently need to retract these accusations, they can print retractions weeks later on the bottom of page 23 of the newspaper where it is unlikely to be noticed.

In addition, the manipulators in the media intentionally ignore or downplay transgressions and prevarications on behalf of the people they agree with while making an enormous fanfare about any imperfections found in their perceived enemies.

The media hated George W. Bush and made a big deal about the victory pose he assumed during the Iraqi war on the deck of a battleship with a sign behind him declaring, "Mission Accomplished." Of course that war went on for several more years with many casualties and enormous expenditures of taxpayer dollars. The same media has largely ignored the fact that Barack Obama stated that with the death of Osama bin Laden and the drone strikes of several other Al Qaeda leaders that we were winning the war and our enemies were on the run. If anything, Al Qaeda is becoming stronger with many people vying for the leadership role. Also, the same media that portrayed Watergate as the scandal of the century sat quietly by as the current administration proclaimed the IRS harassment of the administration's enemies "a phony scandal." By not focusing on the "fast and furious" scandal, the Benghazi debacle, the IRS scandal, the government surveillance revelations, and so on, the hope is that the public will simply forget about these horrendous shortcomings and move on. This will work only if American voters remain uneducated.

What Does a Good Education Look Like?

I recently visited the College of the Ozarks in Branson, Missouri. Like Berea College in Kentucky, they require all students to work at least fifteen hours per week. Their nickname, Hard Work University, is well earned. They are a Christian college that is both true to its convictions and selective—they only accept one out of ten applicants. They are definitely not politically correct and place strong emphasis on the founding principles of our nation and on Christian doctrine. The students, faculty, and administrators are the most courteous and friendly people you could ever hope to meet. One might say these students are being indoctrinated the right way. They are taught fiscal responsibility and all graduate with no debt.

If we don't start following the College of the Ozarks' example of teaching our young people about the values and principles that made our nation great, those values and principles will be replaced by something else that is unlikely to be inspiring and elevating. We have to be just as proactive as the secular progressives who have put us in the position we are in now and have been over the last few decades. We must not be ashamed of who we are or what we believe, in fact we should be extremely proud of our historical accomplishments. There is no room for gloating, but we must remember that if we don't put appropriate facts and people before our young people, someone else will substitute their version of *Utopia*.

To be successful we must take politics out of education and concentrate on empowering the entire American populace. This is the only way that the people's will can be ensured so that we can have the kind of nation that was envisioned by our founders. We must take advantage of all the educational tools available to return us to a place where our public education system is the envy of the world. The rapid development of virtual classrooms and smart computers that are able tutors can be a godsend that will be well worth the cost, enabling us to be serious about our obligation to educate people. Part of that education includes preparing people for jobs of the future, which will decrease unemployment and increase fulfillment while brightening future generations' prospects. Last, we should shine the bright light of truth on the forces of manipulation that run rampant throughout our society today. Improvements in education, combined with wisdom and knowledge, would then turn our country around.

Action Steps

1. Challenge yourself to learn a new fact about American history each day for one month.
2. Resolve to replace television and Internet surfing with reading for a month.
3. Learn the names of your state and federal government representatives and research their voting records.
4. Cross-reference each use of statistics in a news report to determine whether the reporter is spinning the facts.

12

WISDOM AND KNOWLEDGE

How much better to get wisdom than gold, and understanding
than silver!

PROVERBS 16:16

When I was in medical school, a prized possession was a copy
of the last year's examination in the various courses. Many students would memorize the questions and answers from previous years and feel that they had a significant advantage at exam
time only to discover that they answered incorrectly on numerous occasions. They were culling the old exams for knowledge,
but not using wisdom in the process.

Wise persons would understand that the professors knew
that students would acquire old exams and try to remember the
correct answers. They would also realize that professors tend to
be smart people and would likely slip in something that would
change the question ever so slightly, requiring a different answer. The wise students really didn't care very much about the
previous year's answer, but spent a lot of time analyzing the
question to determine what body of knowledge they would

need to correctly answer such a question. They would then make sure that they had a thorough understanding of that body of information, recognizing that it is important and would be tested for again. Needless to say, those students tended to do very well. Without a doubt, students who did poorly were very knowledgeable and generally had been high achievers throughout their lives, but they were looking for a quick solution without fully understanding and dissecting the questions.

Not Just the Facts

Many people use the terms *wisdom* and *knowledge* interchangeably. They are, however, quite different, and having one in no way confers the other. Knowledge is familiarity with facts. The more knowledge one has, the more things one is capable of doing, but only with wisdom is one able to discern which of the many things they are capable of doing should be pursued and in what order.

Wisdom is essentially the same thing as common sense, the slight difference is that common sense provides the ability to react appropriately, while wisdom is frequently more proactive and additionally encourages the shaping of the environment. As such, wisdom is the most important commodity for anyone who is planning to be successful in any endeavor.

Solomon, the son of King David in the Bible, is considered by many to be the wisest man who ever lived. His wisdom led to great wealth and renown. Many will remember that his first challenge as king of Israel was to determine what to do in the case of two women who came before him, both claiming to be the mother of the same baby. Had he based his decision on knowledge alone, King Solomon would have focused on the women's testimony by interrogating them. Instead, after hearing all the arguments, King Solomon declared that a swordsman should split the baby and give half to each woman. One of the women thought that was a fair solution and the other was horrified and immediately relinquished her claim on the baby. In his wisdom, he used his knowledge that the real mother would truly love the baby and prefer to give it to the other woman rather than killing it.

You've probably noticed that I frequently quote Solomon, the writer of the Book of Proverbs in the Bible. Since the day that I tried to stab another teenager, I have started and ended each day reading from the Book of Proverbs, which was instrumental on that particular day in helping me realize how foolishly I had been acting. I also believe that God has a sense of humor, because he inspired my parents to give me the middle name of Solomon knowing that I would have this great affinity for the Book of Proverbs, one of the greatest repositories of wisdom. Like Solomon, I, too, gained great notoriety as a surgeon who divided babies, who in this case were conjoined at the head.

Even though my mother had very little formal education and thus little knowledge, she was extremely observant and very wise. Since she worked as a domestic in the homes of very successful people, she decided to observe how they managed their lives to achieve success. She compared their actions with those of the many unsuccessful people who populated our surroundings, and after careful analysis concluded that the big difference was reading and studying. Hence her insistence that my brother and I read two books per week. Although this move was quite unpopular, it yielded tremendous results for both my brother, Curtis, and me. My mother's wisdom prompted her to use the little knowledge she had to greatly benefit her sons.

While wisdom dictates the need for education, education does not necessarily make one wise. I remember a man when I was growing up who was extremely well educated and had two master's degrees. He could wax eloquently on many subjects but had a very difficult time sustaining himself economically. In fact, he would frequently mooch off of anyone who would take pity on him. On the other hand, many of the greatest achievers in our society never finished college. That includes Bill Gates Jr., Steve Jobs, and Dan Snyder, who is the owner of the Washington Redskins. This does not mean that higher education isn't highly desirable and beneficial, but it does indicate that the wise use of knowledge is more important than knowledge itself.

As my wife and I traveled around the country over the last few months, we encountered large and enthusiastic crowds, many of whom feel that I should run for public office. I believe what they are really clamoring for is not me per se, but for the return of common sense and intelligible speech to solve our ever-increasing problems.

Many Experts Lack Wisdom

It is always interesting to watch the "experts" expound on various topics from the economy to national defense to social issues, and so on, sometimes presenting a host of statistics and little-known studies as proof of their expertise. They claim that their knowledge and all those letters behind their name give them unquestionable authority to declare truth. Some of these experts continue to claim that our economy remains sluggish because we are not borrowing and spending at a greater rate. They want another stimulus package and if that doesn't work, I can guarantee you they will want yet another. I will admit that these people are very knowledgeable, but I severely doubt that they possess wisdom. I believe my mother with her third-grade education could come up with a better plan than theirs. When someone does challenge them, they love to say, "That person is not an expert and can't possibly know what she's talking about."

I have to chuckle when some of them say that "Ben Carson is a neurosurgeon and can't possibly know anything about economics." Many of these same people were involved in crafting the Affordable Care Act even though their training is not in health care. They say that economic principles have broad application and therefore their recommendations are legitimate. I say that common sense has broad application and can be used in all areas. In fact, I would choose common sense over knowledge in almost every circumstance. I also like to point out that five physicians signed the Declaration of Independence, our founding document, and they certainly were not shy about expressing their views regarding the principles that should govern our nation.

A Vision for a Wiser Health Care System

As a doctor, I believe I have acquired some wisdom that can be applied to our need for a well-functioning health care system for the nation. The agenda needs to be the health of the people as opposed to a political feather in a cap, and being a doctor, I would make that a priority more naturally than would a politician. Unfortunately, the Affordable Care Act was more of a victory for the Obama administration than for the American people.

In order to have good health care, you need a patient and a health care provider. Originally, the middleman facilitated the relationship between a person and their doctor, but now the middleman is the primary entity, with the health care provider and the patient at his beck and call. The middleman gains financially by denying health care to clients, even when they are supposed to be facilitating the health care process. The whole system is upside down and it is no wonder that it is dysfunctional.

If we are to reform the system, we must know what the overriding goals of reform are. First, not only do we need to stop the rapid rise of health care costs, we need to decrease these costs. Second, we need to make sure that everyone has access to basic health care. Third, we need to restore the doctor-patient relationship and put patients back in charge of their own health. (These are not given in order of importance.)

As I said at the National Prayer Breakfast, I believe everyone should have a health savings account (HSA) and an electronic medical record (EMR) at the time of birth as a first step toward reform. The EMR should only be in the patient's possession in the form of an electronic chip embedded into a card or device that can be shared with a health care provider at the patient's discretion. It would not be available to the IRS or any other governmental agency, and the database would of course need to be as secure as possible to protect personal information from hackers. The HSA could be populated with funds supplied by an employer, the owner, relatives, friends, and governmental sources.

Since we already spend twice as much per capita on health care in America as does any other country in the world, even if we put substantial monies in everyone's HSA, there's a strong possibility that our shared national health care cost would still decrease. Because there are many responsible individuals and employers who would be willing to contribute to the HSA's, it would only be necessary for the government to make contributions in the cases of individuals incapable of making a living. In Singapore, the government deducts regular contributions to the medical savings accounts from each worker's paycheck. Singapore is capable of providing excellent medical care for all citizens for less than a quarter of what we pay.

With each person owning his own HSA in the United States, most people would become interested in saving by shopping for the most cost-effective high-quality health care plans available. This would bring the entire health care industry into the free-market economic model resulting in price transparency and creating a system where services and pricing are more closely related to value. In our current third-party insurance-based health-care payment system, it would not be unusual to find a hospital in one part of town that charges $66,000 for an appendectomy while in the same city another hospital charges only $14,000 for the same operation. Since a third party is responsible for the payments, the patient doesn't really care which of the two hospitals is used, and spends an unnecessarily large amount of money.

Approximately 80 percent of all encounters between the health care provider and the patient in a system where HSAs are widely used would be covered by the private account with no need to involve a third party. Since most of the relationships would be doctor-patient relationships, the doctors certainly would not order things without regard to price, and patients would not permit excessive depletion of their HSA's by careless expenditure. With everybody becoming cost conscious, price transparency would be of paramount importance and fair competition would cause prices to be consistent and reasonable.

It is natural to ask what happens if a man needs an operation and does not have enough money in his HSA to cover the cost? The system would be designed in such a way that allows members of his immediate family to shift money from their HSA accounts to his without any penalties. In essence, this would make each family unit its own private health insurance company with no unnecessary middleman increasing costs. I would also make it possible for people to pass the money in their HSAs to family members at the time of their death. This would largely eliminate incentive to spend the money in the account in order not to lose it.

A portion of the money in the account could be used to purchase bridge or catastrophic insurance, which would be relatively inexpensive since it would only be used for those 20 percent of cases too expensive to be covered by the typical HSA account. This would work in a manner similar to homeowners insurance that has a high deductible. If that homeowners insurance was used for every type of repair needed on the home with little or no deduction, the cost would be astronomical. Since it is used only for major and expensive home repairs and because routine repairs are taken care of primarily by the homeowner, the cost is reasonable.

The HSA accounts would only be for bona fide medical purposes and the money could not be borrowed and/or legally used for any other reason. Special precautions would be in place to oversee the accounts of addicts and other people who have proven themselves to be fiscally irresponsible. In the case of individuals who are mentally incapacitated, a trustworthy family member would likely be appointed as guardian of their HSA account. It could also be made possible for any adult to donate up to a certain predetermined amount of money from their account to any other person's account for charitable reasons. This becomes an easy way for churches and other organizations to provide charity care at their discretion. It also would encourage those people with massive amounts of money in their accounts to think charitably toward others.

This system would put people back in charge of their own health care, bring down costs, and eliminate massive regulatory bureaucratic nightmares for both patients and providers.

Tort reform on a national basis would be an essential part of this plan. When doctors have to practice defensive medicine, some procedures are done and tests are ordered purely for medicolegal reasons. Virtually every other nation in the world has figured out a way to take care of patients who suffer as a result of attempts by medical personnel to help them. I practiced in Australia for one year as a neurosurgeon, and my malpractice premiums were only $200 a year at that time. Compare this with the $300,000 malpractice insurance fee assessed on a litigation-free neurosurgeon in Philadelphia today.

The quality of neurosurgical care in Australia was excellent just as it is in America, but at that time it was difficult or impossible to bring a medical malpractice lawsuit against someone on a contingency basis. In other words, you had to take money out of your own pocket in order to sue someone, which meant you were unlikely to do that unless you had a very good case. In our system you can sue and pay little or nothing while engaging in activities that might make you a millionaire. It certainly should come as no surprise to anyone that certain lawyers and patients alike would want to take advantage of such a medical lottery.

We need to have a national system that allows immediate and appropriate compensation for medical injuries. If a particular practitioner is responsible on a regular basis for patient compensation due to inappropriate care, that information would be available as a public record and savvy consumers who were vigilant regarding the distribution of their HSA dollars would be unlikely to frequent such practitioners. Retraining or disciplinary actions might also be easier to enact. This is another example of how the free market can be a positive force in ensuring excellence.

I am currently working with other health care providers and legislators to incorporate these ideas into a truly affordable health care plan that is relatively simple and puts patients and doctors back in charge of health care. It is vital that we emphasize the importance of working together in a bipartisan fashion, because sickness and disease have no party affiliation, nor should those who are trying to conquer them. If Obamacare continues to crumble and/or is defunded, no one should gloat or say, "I told you so." This is not a time to proclaim victory, but rather a time to put aside our differences and solve a difficult problem.

In the meantime, I have frequently expressed doubts about the wisdom of imposing a gigantic governmental program like Obamacare without first testing its components. Common sense would dictate a piecemeal implementation of such a massive program since it profoundly affects virtually every American family. As the program is being rolled out, even its most fanatical supporters are starting to see major flaws and losing their enthusiasm for what is destined to be a disaster.

Many promises were made about the program including the famous presidential promise that "If you like your current insurance, you can keep it." On an almost weekly basis we hear about organizations that are dropping or altering the insurance they offer and about health care providers who are retiring or changing the way they practice. This means that millions of Americans who were satisfied with their health care plans now have to make costly and worrisome changes. Many who previously had health care insurance have been demoted to part-time status, so not only do they lose their insurance, but they lose substantial income. The very fact that everyone is looking for exclusions so they don't have to participate right away should be a red flag to any objective observer.

Learn from Mistakes

One of the prime indicators of wisdom is the ability to see a mistake and back away while learning from it. As Proverbs says, "As a dog returns to its vomit, so a fool repeats his foolishness." Ideology frequently renders one incapable of learning and instead makes its ideologues expert excuse makers. They always have someone or something to blame for the failure of their ideas, which in their opinion can't possibly be flawed in any way. You will hardly ever hear the words "I'm sorry," or "I was wrong" coming from their lips. When you see people who fit this description, common sense should tell you they are not to be trusted. Sometimes they are gifted with flowery speech and a pleasant persona, which makes them even more dangerous and misleading, particularly for the trusting souls who want so much to believe in them. There is nothing wrong with wanting desperately to believe in someone or some idea, but the application of common sense should tell anyone with a modicum of objectivity that if that person or those ideas consistently yield bad results, their allegiance should be reconsidered.

Set Priorities Wisely

Another key characteristic of wisdom is the ability to prioritize. One must have perspective in order to know which things are most important. Several administrations have talked about the importance of energy independence, yet we remain as dependent on foreign oil as we were years ago. This is because of a problem with priorities. The Environmental Protection Agency feels it has a duty to protect every aspect of the environment under all circumstances, and that priority has been placed above energy independence.

It is estimated that the amount of oil in the Dakotas and Montana is eight times greater than the amount of oil in Saudi Arabia. Yet the EPA has made it difficult for us to take advantage of the enormous amounts of shale oil available in that area of our nation because of pollution problems, and our government has not done much to find a new solution.

With the knowledge of the shale oil and the problems, a wise overseer would be encouraging the development of safe and clean ways to take advantage of this energy bounty rather than trying to shut down proponents of its use. If you were a seller of jewels and decided to extract them from a cave by using dynamite, but then discovered that the jewels would be ruined by the dynamite blast, you could just give up and say these dynamite blasts destroy air quality and don't yield quality jewels. Or if you were wise, you could say let's look for better and safer ways to extract a valuable commodity.

I thoroughly believe that we have a duty to protect our environment not only for ourselves but for the next generations. However, we also have a duty to develop our economic potential and free ourselves of unnecessary stress and dependency on volatile foreign sources of energy. As a bonus, energy independence for us means decreased revenues for radical terrorist elements who aim to destroy our way of life. Wisdom would lead us to find solutions reflecting those priorities.

Humility Comes Before Wisdom

How does one acquire wisdom? First and foremost, one must be humble enough to recognize that one doesn't know everything. "The more you know, the less you know." This saying means that a wise person understands that on any given issue, there is still much knowledge to be acquired, while the foolish glory in their limited knowledge. It is essential for the prosperity of our nation that our leaders be endowed with knowledge and wisdom.

The acquisition of knowledge is relatively straightforward, but wisdom has to be sought prayerfully from many sources. First, anyone who is trying to live her life wisely should imitate my mother and observe carefully what is going on around her.

If you can learn from the triumphs and mistakes of others, you can move further and faster along the path of success. Second, you can also learn a great deal from your own failures if you are willing to admit failure. Finally and most important, consult God, the source of all wisdom. I ask God for wisdom and guidance on a daily basis, and His answers were instrumental during my surgical career, especially when dealing with situations that were unique and extraordinarily complex. His wisdom is at least equally important in my retirement. Pray for wisdom and believe that you will receive a positive answer to that request as the Bible commands in James 1:5. He always provides what is necessary and will guide us in the best way to serve Him and love our neighbors.

Action Steps

1. Ask an older and wiser person for his or her perspective on a controversial issue.
2. Read the first four chapters of the Book of Proverbs in the Bible this week. Glean the wisdom that is there for the taking.
3. Think of a recent mistake you made and determine to learn from it.
4. Consider your priorities—should you be spending your time differently?

13

MY BROTHER'S KEEPER

Those who oppress the poor insult their Maker, but those who help the poor honor Him.

PROVERBS 14:31

In the mid-1960s my aunt Jean and uncle William were finally able to escape the inner city of Boston and move to a rural home in the town of Holly, Michigan. They had lived in Michigan before moving to Boston a decade earlier and had always dreamed about returning home. Uncle William still had a lot of friends in Michigan and under his supervision, and with a lot of backbreaking effort, they were able to build a reasonable home.

Uncle William had a brother by the name of Albert who was developmentally disabled, or retarded, as they used to say. There was no possibility of Albert's ever being able to care for himself and my uncle felt it was his responsibility to make sure that all of Albert's basic needs were met. He and my aunt constructed a small home on the property for Albert, and he was pretty reclusive. Even though Albert could not read, write, or even communicate in a way that most people understood, he was capable of hard work, including transporting heavy objects, loading and unloading trucks, and other activities where brawn was more important than brains. Albert was always proud when he put in a good day of labor and he enjoyed a good meal. He trusted Uncle William and was very obedient.

The children, including yours truly, were frightened of Albert at first, but as time went on we got to know that he was actually quite benign and very shy. By the time I went off to college at Yale, I had grown quite fond of Albert and my girlfriend Candy, who later became my wife, liked him also.

Albert had never worked outside of the home nor had served in the military, so there was no source of public assistance to help with his care. My relatives never complained about the care they provided for Albert and in fact they felt it was their duty.

My aunt and uncle are examples of a mind-set that seems to be dying out in recent years. Until recently, it was expected in America that families would take care of their own disabled or poor, regardless of whether the government provided any assistance. There was a strong sense of responsibility for family and neighbors in need, a sense that unfortunately is much rarer today. Instead of caring for the disabled and elderly, many Americans expect the government to care for them, resulting in a lowered standard of care and a ballooning national debt. Compounding the problem, many others have embraced models of government assistance that actually push the poor into deeper cycles of poverty. Until these patterns are broken, our nation will continue to decline.

Socialism: A Deterrent to Charity

In many socialist societies the basic needs of the elderly and poor are provided by the state. This is expensive, a problem that is partially resolved by denying certain medical treatments to the elderly. Socialism demands that every member of society have their basic needs provided for by the government, but it is nearly impossible to stay ahead of the expanding costs in this type of governing structure so the citizens become enslaved by governmental debt.

Does capitalism offer a better solution? The answer is a resounding yes, as long as personal responsibility and compassion are included. Capitalism practiced without such elements has given the entire idea of a free market a bad rap, when in reality, every economic system is insufficient and undesirable when it is devoid of virtue. Capitalism certainly should not mean "every man for himself" but should instead allow every man to freely earn and freely share with his neighbor.

Respectful Care for the Elderly

Caring for one's family is a basic responsibility that is becoming increasingly crucial in today's economy. Rapidly shifting population demographics indicate a need to reconsider how we care for the elderly in our nation. Less than half of the population can now look forward to a comfortable retirement at age sixty-five because retirement plans have been derailed by a stagnant economy with no signs of a lasting and meaningful recovery. Many older couples can certainly pay their mortgage, car notes, utility bills, and supply food and some level of entertainment without much difficulty as long as they continue to work. With the job market undergoing many changes, it will be hard for many elderly individuals who do not have appropriate skills to keep up and they may be forced into retirement.

Unfortunately, the proliferation of nursing homes and elder care facilities in our society indicates that many families are reluctant to exercise enough compassion to care for their own parents and relatives. In some cases people must work outside the home to earn a living and have relatives who cannot be left alone, and these cases are understandable, but those who expect others to care for their parents and don't even visit them should remember that these people took care of them when they could not care for themselves.

In cases where the problem is due more to circumstances rather than lack of character, we need to work together to find solutions. The task of providing full-time care for the elderly or disabled has become progressively more difficult in families where everyone is working outside the home and no one can be a full-time guardian for the person(s) in need. Fortunately, there is an old saying that "necessity is the mother of invention." The importance of caring for one's own remains unchanged, and our society needs to create new ways of doing this.

In some ways, this is already happening. A whole new industry known as adult day care arose because of this necessity. It has created many jobs and provided a stimulating and safe environment for millions of elderly and incapacitated individuals. Many of these adult day care centers are independently owned and operated with little or no assistance from the government. Community living with the ability to pool and share resources can provide a healthy social environment while reducing financial obligations. A variety of such communities can be built around the nation quite economically, allowing freedom and peace of mind to those who deserve a period of relaxation in their lives. These are the kinds of organizations that should be encouraged as time goes on, particularly in light of the growing number of elderly individuals in our society. If we just depend on government programs as the number of elders increases faster than our young population, it will accelerate our rate of debt accumulation, which will negatively affect us all.

We also need to encourage everyone to feel a responsibility toward taking care of their elderly parents and disabled relatives. It should be anticipated that the day will come when it will be necessary to do this, as it probably will be for each of us to be taken care of by sons and daughters, nieces and nephews, in-laws, or other relatives in the future. This care can be expensive, but it is not nearly as costly as nursing homes and other full-time care facilities. If these expenses are anticipated and resources are set aside accordingly, undue hardship and guilt can frequently be avoided.

I know there will be some people saying, "I can barely care for my own needs, how can anyone expect me to provide for someone else, even if they are my parents?" During the time in America when these kinds of questions were not asked, people didn't necessarily have to have multiple vehicles, flat screen televisions, multiple cell phones, iPads, and a host of other "necessities." This begs the question: Is it more important to take care of your extended family or have the creature comforts pop culture demands?

Compassion for the Poor

Anyone familiar with the Bible knows that our responsibilities to care for others don't end with our families. There are numerous Biblical references to our obligations to care for the poor and to love our neighbors as ourselves. And even if you don't believe in God and/or the Bible, there are commonsense reasons to exercise compassion toward the poor. Most of us have an innate sense that it is right to care for those less fortunate than ourselves, and even those with the hardest hearts should understand that elevating the social status of the poor is better for the economy as a whole.

Compassion, however, should mean providing a mechanism to escape poverty rather than simply maintaining people in an impoverished state by supplying handouts. By doing this we give them an opportunity to elevate their personal situations, which eventually decreases our need to take care of them and empowers them to be able to exercise compassion toward others.

The Problem of Government Dependency

Having established that we should care about our neighbors, the next question is who is my neighbor and where does my responsibility end, leaving the government in charge? My answer will come as a great surprise to many, but I do not believe the government has any obligation to take care of able-bodied citizens who are capable of providing for themselves. Private citizens, on the other hand, should be encouraged but not coerced to provide as much aid and opportunities to their neighbors as they are capable of. Indiscriminately providing for the needs of people who can provide for themselves is not only unwise, it is cruel because it tends in many cases to create dependency and robs people of their God-given dignity.

The only reason I can imagine that it would be a good idea for government to foster dependency in large groups of citizens is to cultivate a dependable voting bloc that will guarantee continued power as long as the entitlements are provided. The problem of course is that such a government will eventually "run out of other people's money," as Margaret Thatcher once famously said.

The Value of the Minimum-Wage Job

As I mentioned earlier, it is quite possible to obtain more money from the welfare system than one would get from a minimum-wage job. It is hard to criticize someone who takes advantage of such a situation. The problem with this line of thinking is that it relegates the value of job experience to a lowly position on the totem pole.

I have had many jobs on the way to becoming a physician, all of which provided some knowledge and skill sets that were useful, no matter how low-skilled and low-paid they were. My first jobs were as a lab assistant both in high school and at Wayne State University in Detroit, where I learned concepts such as sterility and how to set up laboratory experiments. During the summer between high school and college, I obtained a job as a payroll office clerk at the Ford Motors world headquarters, where I learned about many office machines and how to operate them. Next I had a job as a bank teller, where I learned accuracy and efficiency as well some things about dealing with bank robbers. A job as a mailroom clerk taught me various ways of efficient filing and delivery, and a job as an encyclopedia salesman taught me much about presentation. One of my best experiences was as a supervisor for highway cleanup crews. I learned how to motivate individuals who were not interested in working and I learned the importance of teamwork in the generation of an efficient workforce.

My experience as an assembly line worker in an automobile factory taught me the importance of concentration, and my job as a student aid to the Yale University campus police gave me an opportunity to learn a great deal about security for a large organization. With that job there were also a lot of perks, like being able to get into concerts free of charge. And I derived great benefit from my job as an X-ray technician between my first and second years in medical school. Learning how to operate that equipment led to a subsequent new technique for visualizing a difficult part of the skull that facilitated a complex neurosurgical procedure. Later in life as an attending neurosurgeon, occasions would arise when X-rays had to be taken in the operating room and all the X-ray technicians were tied up elsewhere. I was able to save a great deal of time by being able to operate the equipment myself, which typically amazed the operating room staff.

I also had a job as a crane operator in a steel factory that helped me realize that I was gifted with great eye-hand coordination, a fact that later affected my career choice. Finally, a job as a school bus driver taught me to be extremely cautious around small schoolchildren.

On the surface it might appear that many of these jobs had

nothing to do with a successful career as a neurosurgeon, but closer analysis should lead one to the understanding that no knowledge is wasted knowledge. It can be used in virtually any career, and opens many doors of opportunity.

I don't wish to sound cold, but sitting around collecting welfare checks is unlikely to bolster one's résumé and expose one to job opportunities. When you make yourself valuable by acquiring knowledge and many skills, you make yourself more employable. Even if no one wants to hire you, you can create your own job. Being able to cut a lawn, weed a lawn, or garden, cook, clean, paint, wash cars, pick fruits and vegetables, and so on may not make you a millionaire, but certainly can pay the bills and put food on the table if you are not extravagant.

Sometimes one has to be humble enough to start at the bottom with a minimum-wage job even if you have a college degree. Once you get your foot in the door, you can prove your worth and rapidly move up the ladder. If you never get in the door, it is unlikely that you will rise to the top.

I have no doubt that there are millions of extremely talented and intelligent people who have dropped out of the labor force and are living on the dole. They are not counted as unemployed, which makes the government happy, because it can claim that the jobless numbers are improving. These people are doing no one, including themselves, a favor by depriving the labor force of their potential contributions. If you know such individuals, please share this chapter with them and encourage them to go out and make the American dream come true in their lives— that is one way of being your brother's keeper.

Rolling Back Welfare

One logical and compassionate solution to the problem of growing welfare rolls is to set a date several years away for the elimination of welfare payments for able-bodied individuals who could work and support themselves. This would give them time to prepare for the job market and it would also make people much more careful in their family planning. Some liberals would say that is mean and heartless, but some conservatives would say that continuing to sustain people in a dependent position with meager welfare payments is what is really cruel, because it frequently removes the incentive to engage in self-improvement activities.

People (Not Government) Helping People

When it comes to empowering those who have been rendered complacent by an overly generous system that cultivates their votes rather than their talents, churches and other charitable organizations can play an important role. Loving and caring relationships with those in need of jobs and self-esteem can bring hope and encouragement to the downtrodden, especially when combined with examples of success, the provision of opportunities, and training to achieve that success. It's all about people helping people, which is why such organizations exist in the first place and why they have tax-exempt status.

The Reformed Church of Bronxville, New York, has a mentorship program called "Coming Home," which aids formerly incarcerated individuals in their adjustment and acclimation

into society. Dawn Ravella, the director of mission and out-
reach at the church said,

> The idea is to absorb them into a supportive community
> to help with the re-entry process, deal with the trauma and to
> help them get back on their feet. . . . It's so powerful what's
> happening here. We at the church thought we were starting
> this to help other people, and it's been transformational for us.
> This program has been duplicated in at least eight other
> churches in New York City.

And as far as helping the downtrodden, since 2005, 600,000
volunteers have worked 1.4 million man-hours under the auspices
of Samaritan's Purse led by Franklin Graham, helping 24,000
families in 140 disasters across the nation. Also, their "Operation
Heal Our Patriots" program liberates double-amputee veterans,
enabling them to live more normal lives.

Some people are not religious and do not believe that religion
is helpful, but hopefully such people are desirous of helping their
fellow citizens achieve success in their lives. There is absolutely
no reason why they cannot cooperate with churches and community organizations in a synergistic fashion to once again
achieve a growing and vital economy that offers people a hand
up rather than a handout.

I am particularly fond of churches because they are supposed to show kindness toward others, and if they do not, they
can be embarrassed when that is pointed out to them, resulting
in renewed efforts to help others. Other types of organizations,
especially government agencies, are frequently staffed by people
who only see it as a job, know they have job security, and there-

fore treat people without respect or compassion. If I had the authority to do so, I would plant random observers around governmental employees who could record their pattern of behavior and dismiss without recourse those people who manifested consistently unacceptable behavior. I believe that would quickly alter the nonchalant attitudes of government employees. I also believe that these employees would feel better about their jobs and themselves with the application of kindness and compassion to their daily chores.

What About Those Who Won't Take Responsibility?

I can't leave this topic without talking about those individuals in our society who are completely and utterly irresponsible. Who is responsible for taking care of those who have no intention of taking care of themselves? If they are not devoid of mental faculties, it is safe to assume that their behavior pattern is learned and that it can be unlearned by allowing them to experience the consequences of their choices. This is one of the ways that children are taught to be responsible and I believe it is a technique that will also work for adults who act like children.

Those who are horrified at such a suggestion should feel perfectly free to take these individuals under their wings and care for their needs. I believe in grace and am grateful for the undeserved mercy that I have received, especially mercy that forced me to better myself. However, to thrust this responsibility of caring for them on everyone else is unfair and encourages others to adopt similar irresponsible lifestyles.

We should be dedicated to providing for all of our citizens

life, liberty, and the pursuit of happiness. That means giving them the opportunity to pursue any course of action they choose for the purpose of bringing fulfillment to their lives, assuming it is legal. In no reasonable way can our responsibility as a society be interpreted as providing for the needs of all citizens, especially if they are ones who by choice make no attempt to provide for themselves. Again, this applies only to individuals who are fully capable of taking care of themselves.

True Compassion—A Rare Thing

Unfortunately, both Republican and Democratic politicians will have objections to the proposals I have made. I have heard some conservatives say all of us should have enough sense to adequately prepare for our retirement and if we fail to do so, we should have to suffer the consequences. Although there may be some merit to this sentiment, it does not show compassion. We are all human beings with shortcomings, therefore whenever we are capable of helping someone in need, we should do so even if his own mistakes produced the need, because this is what we would want them to do if the situation were reversed. I have heard some liberals say we have an obligation to fully take care of everyone regardless of lifestyle and poor choices. This lack of tough love encourages more irresponsible behavior and a progressively larger number of people to care for until all resources are exhausted. This seems compassionate, but instead is cruel like anything else that fosters dependency.

In short, yes, we are our brothers' keepers, but we have to be smart in the way that we keep them, and the compassion we show must be in consideration of the long term, with a defined purpose of providing life, liberty, and the pursuit of happiness.

Action Steps

1. Check on an elderly relative or friend this week.
2. Go out of your way to help a stranger this week.
3. Commit a percentage of your time for volunteer work at a local charity this month.
4. Find out what your church or religious organization is doing for your community.

PART THREE

—

WHO WE ARE

14

WITHOUT A VISION

When people do not accept divine guidance, they run wild.
But whoever obeys the law is happy.

PROVERBS 29:18

When I was in middle school I was friends with a nice young man named Charlie, who served as a punching bag for many of the other students, including the class bully, Randy. One day when the teacher was not in the room, Randy beat Charlie and began strangling him. Many of the other students gasped in horror and thought that they were going to witness a murder. Fortunately, Randy came to his senses and desisted from his attack. Charlie was visibly shaken but continued with his nonconfrontational demeanor until one day one of the smaller boys attacked him and he decided to fight back. Not only did he win the fight but he completely dominated the contest, leaving the other boy in a state of total humiliation that was well deserved. That day marked a turning point in Charlie's life and he became a completely different person. His confidence grew and people stopped picking on him. He also became a much better student and went on to become very successful in high school.

Charlie's metamorphosis occurred when he faced significant trials in his life head-on. His ordeal strengthened him, and his victory gave him a different vision for his life. He did not necessarily become a combatant, but he gained enough self-confidence to be able to live his life without fear. Once he had a glimpse of how good life could be out from under a bully's thumb, he began to take himself seriously. What happened with Charlie undoubtedly gave me the courage to resist a bully later in my life. Without his example, I might not have known it would be possible to stand up for myself, to envision a life free of being bullied.

Bullying by the British was a major impetus for the resistance movement that resulted in our ultimate independence and the establishment of our Constitution. An even bigger role was played in the establishment of a national vision by the desire for freedom. Our founders saw themselves as free people who could pursue whatever dreams inspired them. However, success is never achieved by people who only dream and do not act. My wife and I have some close friends who are examples of this truth. The husband was an attorney and the wife was an elementary school teacher. She was constantly talking about her dream of becoming a lawyer but she never really pursued that dream. I remember saying to her one day, "Just do it and stop dreaming." I reminded her that it only takes three years to complete law school and that three years goes by quite rapidly. She has been a successful attorney for many years and has established quite a reputation. Our founders were able to conquer their fears and act on their dreams on the way to establishing a spectacular vision for America. They embedded that vision in the Constitution of the United States of America and intended for that document to be revered and held up as a guidepost for a truly free society.

Proverbs 29:18 (NKJV) says, "Without a vision the people perish." If a society doesn't have a shared understanding of its goals, it cannot move forward. To aimlessly drift along while reacting to events is a recipe for disaster. As Americans, we have the vision of our founders, codified in the Constitution and lived out by citizens who worked together, as a heritage. Unless we recover our lost vision, communicate it simply to the next generation, and seek out visionary leaders, our country will remain in serious trouble.

The Constitution as Vision

During the American Revolution, the colonies differed from one another in many ways but had a shared vision of liberation from a dominating British monarch. Each of the states had different mechanisms for achieving economic success and they had different feelings about the institution of slavery, but their overwhelming desire was to be able to pursue their dreams without outside interference. They were wise enough to recognize that their chances of success would be greatly enhanced if they worked together.

In 1787, the union almost split apart due to what were thought to be irreconcilable differences. It took the wise words of the senior statesman, Benjamin Franklin, to reinstate unity with his recommendation of prayer. He and other leaders were subsequently able to help frame one of the most concise and inspirational national visions ever crafted, namely, the U.S. Constitution.

The Constitution was written primarily to protect the rights of the people and not the rights of the government to rule the people. It restrains the natural tendencies of government to expand while disregarding the rights of its constituents. Our freedoms are safe as long as we abide by its principles.

Drifting Away

Unfortunately, the executive, judicial, and legislative branches of government have become increasingly concerned with their image and their political parties, have drifted away from strict interpretations of the Constitution, and have substituted their own ideologies for the original vision. As a result, our government produces massively complicated taxation schemes, impossibly intricate and uninterpretable health care laws, and other intrusive measures instead of being a watchful guardian of our rights. Instead of providing an environment that allows diligent people to thrive on the basis of their own hard work and entrepreneurship, our government has taken on the role of trying to care for everyone's needs and redistributing the fruits of everyone's labors in a way consistent with its own ideology.

A New Utopian Vision?

Under this new vision for America, lawmakers are not particularly concerned with the people's will, since they firmly believe that they know better than the people. Confident in the superiority of their ideas, they cram measures like the Affordable Care

Act down the throats of protesting citizens and then have the nerve to tell the people that they'll like it once they understand it. This kind of paternal attitude is changing us from a representative type of governmental structure to a nanny state, where the government tells the constituency what's good for them and monitors and regulates every aspect of their lives.

The vision of this new form of government is a society where the basic needs of everyone are provided and no one needs to fret about anything, regardless of whether they choose to work hard and be productive or relax and enjoy life. This is a very attractive vision to those looking for a free ride. It certainly would not have been the kind of vision that hundreds of years ago would have caused many immigrants to cross treacherous seas and leave behind loved ones in order to try to provide a better future for their families.

The United States is not the first nation to alter its vision to include a more communal society, an alteration which on its surface seems like a noble goal. The problems with these utopian goals is that they never work in practice. For the government to be able to distribute goods to everyone, there must be significant production of goods and services. If producers know that the government is going to redistribute the wealth they accumulate, they have little incentive to increase production to meet the demand—they would be working more for the same amount of income. If the government decides to force the producer to manufacture more goods, a new problem arises: It is very difficult for a centralized government to know exactly how much to produce without the signals of a free market. Thus centralized economies usually end up with a mismatch between supply and demand.

Practical problems aside, there are moral problems with redistribution. Thomas Jefferson famously put it similarly when he said, "To take from one, because it is thought his own industry and that of his father's has acquired too much, in order to spare to others, who, or whose fathers, have not exercised equal industry and skill, is to violate arbitrarily the first principle of association, the guarantee to everyone the free exercise of his industry and the fruits acquired by it." The utopian vision of communal societies strongly disagrees with Jefferson's views and would advocate for equitable redistribution to prevent massive accumulation by any one group or poverty by another group. The communal philosophy does not recognize exceptional production by individuals or exceptional nonproduction.

When the vision of the U.S. government included guarding the rights of people but staying out of their way, America was an economic engine more powerful than anything the world had ever witnessed. That engine is still in place, and if the original vision can be restored, that engine could restart and quickly obliterate our national debt while helping our nation reclaim its rightful position of leadership and respect throughout the world. Our ability to care for the indigent would also be considerably enhanced and the number of indigent would be significantly decreased in a thriving job market.

Deep Division

Because of our neglect of the Constitution, it has been a while since the people of America could agree on a national vision. Perhaps the last time was toward the end of the Cold War when our unity and strength radically changed the world's power structure for the better. There was a great deal of unity across party lines and the resultant national vision made us a formidable foe or a powerful ally. Today we are deeply divided along ideological lines, as discussed earlier in the book. As a result, our political climate changes dramatically every time power shifts from one party to another. Massive swings to the right are followed by massive swings to the left, destroying the unity that was our strength.

There are deep and sometimes hostile divisions between those who believe in God and those who are atheists. Even deeper divisions exist between those who believe in personal responsibility and those who believe that there is no problem with government dependency. Many believe that as the world's only superpower the United States should engage in strong international leadership, while others feel strongly that we should adopt a laissez-faire attitude. The right to bear arms versus the concern for public safety has produced a deep chasm as have attitudes about gay marriage, abortion, and other social issues. Every time the pendulum swings it leaves more deeply entrenched people at the extremities of the swing. This exacerbates tensions that used to be relatively minor differences.

Because we have strayed so far from the original intent of our nation's goals, and because philosophical differences are so deep and entrenched, the legitimate question is whether our disparities can be peacefully resolved, resulting in a long-term forward trajectory instead of massive pendulum swings. I believe it is possible for us to adopt a positive direction, but it will require exceptionally wise and courageous leadership.

A Constitutional Convention?

Recently, some radio commentators have suggested the need for another constitutional convention since the last one was more than two hundred years ago. While I would be delighted to see a new convention, I don't believe it is practical due to the size, complexity, dishonesty, and animosity that characterizes our political structure today. Fortunately, our founders were visionary and wise men who could foresee the turmoil we now face and anticipated almost everything that would be destructive to their vision except apathy on behalf of the populace in terms of protecting our freedom.

Revering the Constitution

I believe the only thing that will correct our downward trajectory is the rekindling of the enthusiasm for individual freedom and the reestablishment of the U.S. Constitution as the dominant document of governance. Unless the majority of Americans awaken from their complacency and recognize the threat to their fundamental individual liberties imposed by continued expansion of the federal government, nothing will save us from the fate of all pinnacle nations that have preceded us, those that tolerated political and moral corruption while ignoring fiscal irresponsibility.

We the people have lost the inspiration that produced the "can-do attitude" that was our foremost characteristic. We have capitulated to the forces of ever-expanding governmental control of our lives. But it is not too late for us to change. As a beginning, all American citizens must be familiar with our

Constitution, and they must be brave enough to stand up for its principles even if that makes them temporarily unpopular. They must be willing to share their knowledge with others and encourage frank discussions rather than "going along to get along."

Voting for the Constitution

The last point that I just mentioned is the safeguard that our founders built into our system of government to allow "we the people" to rectify an out-of-control governmental structure. As outraged citizens, we have the power to vote out of office any politician who refuses to uphold the Constitution.

One of the most important steps that must be taken if America is to remain free is stimulation of the large voter base that has basically tuned out of politics. One of the political parties or perhaps a new political party has to be dependable and courageously uphold the Constitution. The fact that the Republican Party in particular often seems to stand for principle, only to cave in to pressure at the last minute, has turned off a huge number of voters. A true reformation of the Republican Party would be a breath of fresh air for those voters. Those voters are also up for grabs for the Democrats if they decide suddenly that they want to be the party of the Constitution. In an ideal world, both parties would desire to uphold the Constitution, and their energies could be spent elsewhere, including solving our nation's problems instead of engaging in ideological squabbles.

Just prior to the start of the American Revolution, and throughout its duration, concerned citizens engaged in self-education and education of others by convening community meetings, often in one another's homes, to discuss the desire for freedom and the threat posed by inaction. The same kinds of meetings were held throughout Europe during and after the Dark Ages in an attempt to keep Christianity alive. Both movements were successful because people became activists and used their collective skills, resources, and intellect to bring about the changes they desired. If Americans would meet together the same way and discuss which candidates would best honor the Constitutional vision, our future's security would be much improved.

In making decisions about who should be replaced, it is important for the people not to be deceived by those politicians who claim that the matters they are dealing with and voting on are too complex for the average citizen to understand. I believe our political role models should be people who understand and revere the U.S. Constitution and are willing to defend it from those who feel it is outdated. We need people who can articulate their beliefs in a way that is easily understandable, and people who are willing to point out who among their compatriots are deviating from the Constitution and why. People who are worried about reelection are terrible representatives, especially when they place reelection above principles. Until we the people learn to identify and support those political role models who truly represent our interests, we can expect continued deterioration of governmental trust and ongoing governmental expansion into every aspect of our lives.

In my opinion, if politicians are unable to explain a law or statute in a way that a seventh grader could understand it, then they don't understand it either and should be provided an opportunity to study after being voted out of office. Anyone who writes a law that cannot be easily understood by an average citizen is not worthy of leadership. The Constitution, which was written by extremely learned men, is quite easy to understand and should serve as a gold standard for the language and size of subsequent legislation that is introduced.

Visionary Leadership

Dynamic national leaders tend to be exceptionally good at painting a clear vision that inspires and motivates the populace. For the United States, George Washington was such a figure. He was extraordinarily brave and disciplined, and inspired confidence in his troops even though the odds of victory were often minuscule. He helped formulate the goals for our nation, which included a degree of personal freedom for all citizens, something rarely witnessed in the world previously. This understanding gave him the fortitude to resist the many calls for him to become a monarch.

The British adversaries of General Washington were used to beating their subjects into submission and treated the colonies like many of the other colonies around the world. But they had no overarching vision, putting them at a distinct disadvantage even though they were the most powerful fighting force in the world at that time, and their opponents were an ill-equipped, ragtag bunch of militiamen.

If today's Americans refuse to give up on the constitutional vision, explain that vision clearly, and elect leaders who will uphold it, we will likewise defeat the powers that would bring our country down.

Action Steps

1. Do you have a personal vision for the rest of your life? If not, stop and write out your lifetime, one-, five-, and ten-year goals.
2. Read the Declaration of Independence and the Constitution.
3. Examine candidates in the next election to see if any are potential visionary leaders.
4. Consider whether freedom or security is most important to you. Do you see the trade-offs between the two?

15

ROLE MODELS

Do not carouse with drunkards and gluttons, for they are on
their way to poverty. Too much sleep clothes a person with
rags. Listen to your father, who gave you life, and don't
despise your mother's experience when she is old.

PROVERBS 23:20-22

As a child in Detroit and Boston, I had a rather limited world-
view. The coolest people around were the drug dealers who
drove big-finned fancy cars with huge white-walled tires, and
always displayed the latest fashions, particularly in footwear and
showy big straw hats. Also highly admired were the people who
had risen to the rank of foreman in one of the many factories
that fueled the burgeoning industrial-based economy. Most of
the kids, including me, did not have a big vision of anything
outside of our small world and being a dealer or foreman would
have been great.

I was never heavily drawn toward drug selling or factory
work, but instead I was fascinated whenever I heard stories
about doctors, especially the ones I heard in church about mis-

181

sionary doctors who lived amazing adventures. My family certainly was not friendly with any doctors, but at the little community hospital in our neighborhood, one could occasionally see a well-dressed and polished physician driving off in a beautiful car. I was always eager to visit a doctor even if it meant getting a shot, and I was magnetically drawn to any doctor show on television, especially Dr. Kildare, who was a general practitioner, and Dr. Ben Casey, who was a neurosurgeon.

As mentioned earlier, in the fifth grade my academic performance was so poor that my mother (with her third-grade education) turned off the television and made us read books. I was rather disgruntled at first, but since I had no choice in the matter I began focusing on the reading so I could get my mother-required book reports done, even though she couldn't read them, which we didn't know. Within a matter of weeks, I began to actually know some of the answers to questions in various classes, which was shocking to the teachers and my classmates, and frankly to me as well.

I started out reading about animals because I love nature. I then moved on to plants and minerals before discovering what really affected me: stories about people. As I read about people of great accomplishment I began to understand that success is no accident that only happens to lucky people. Instead it became clear to me that the person who has the most to do with what happens to you in life is you!

Reading helped me realize that becoming a doctor was definitely within my grasp and that I could make this dream a reality if I was willing to invest the necessary time and effort. My vision was ever before me and buoyed me during times of discouragement. The environment can be a small factor but it pales in comparison with the power of determination to achieve a dream.

I did not like poverty. In fact, I hated it until I began reading those books and realized that I had the power to control my own destiny and did not have to be a victim of circumstances. I know many successful people who grew up in poverty and also came to this realization sometime during their preadolescent years. What happened is that we developed a vision of what our lives could be and began to follow that vision, which required establishing plans and following them. When you have a vision, it is much easier to keep your target in sight and know when you are deviating from the plan.

Our Young People Need Vision

I've discussed how necessary a shared vision is to a country. It is equally important to make sure that the young individuals in the country are given role models, providing an inspiring vision of what their lives can be. As a teenager there was a period of time when I began to "hang out" with a gang after school and into the evening. The leader of the group was older than most of the kids at school because he had failed several grades. He was an extremely cool guy who not only had brass knuckles and a knife but he also possessed a shiny .22 caliber handgun. He demonstrated such extreme confidence that many of us followed him around like little ducklings. He either possessed or had access to cars and motorcycles and he always seemed to be flush with cash. For a kid surrounded by poverty and a sense of helplessness, being around a person like this was exciting and offered a false hope of quick financial security.

Fortunately, my fascination with his lifestyle was short-lived as I became captivated by the lives of great inventors, doctors, and explorers whom I was reading about in the library books. Once again my future was protected by academic pursuits, because that young man and many of his followers subsequently lost their lives to the violent subculture rampant in cities like Detroit.

It is common for young people to be deceived by glamour, power, or wealth when choosing their role models. I should quickly add that some adults are also easily fooled by such things. We have a duty as parents and guardians to strive to influence which people capture our children's imaginations. It means taking an active role in their lives and always being aware of who their friends are and what places they frequent. It also means trying to put them in the presence of people of great accomplishment whom we want them to emulate. These are things that used to be done quite routinely by caring guardians, but now many young people derive their identity from their peer group and their social network, which can be extensive.

Miley Cyrus Is Not a Role Model

If we don't help set role models for our children, the media will provide them—and they will not be the role models who will inspire our children to save America by living lives of wisdom, ambition, humility, and discipline.

Many sports stars are among our young people's heroes, but their character is often cause for concern. For example, before he died, I had an opportunity to have breakfast with Tom Landry, the famous former coach of the Dallas Cowboys. We were talking about many of the spectacular players he had coached over the years, but I was unpleasantly surprised to hear that almost all those players had borrowed money from the coach or from others and were far from leading lives of comfort and productivity. I heard exactly the same story in talking to my friend Tony Dungy, who coached the Indianapolis Colts during their glory days. Many of these players are held up before our young people as great heroes because they can throw or catch a ball or perform some other athletic feat consistently and with great flair. Entertainers similarly are extolled as superior human specimens worthy of our praise, adoration, and attention.

Some of these people possess spectacular talent and I do not begrudge them the millions of dollars they receive for displaying those talents. I am, however, concerned about the godlike status bestowed on them when in most cases their intellectual contributions to the betterment of our society do not justify such deification. Like athletes, many entertainers are here today and gone tomorrow. It is a sad sight wandering through some of the Las Vegas casinos and seeing performers trying to get spectators to remember their glory days. I wish there were a television show that came on every day titled *Lifestyles of the Formerly Rich and Famous*. This would perhaps enable many of our young people to recognize the fleeting nature of some types of fame and begin to focus on developing their God-given intellectual talents so they can make a contribution to the betterment of society.

This is not to say that we don't need and value athletes and entertainers but we need to bring perspective to the table when talking about these kinds of careers. For example, only seven in one million will become starters in the NBA. Less than 1 percent of student athletes attending college will have a career in professional sports due to the limited number of available slots. The average career span of a professional athlete is less than five years, and only one in ten thousand makes it in a lasting way in the entertainment field. Despite these discouraging odds, thousands of people dedicate themselves to being one of the few, while often neglecting preparation for the assumption of key productive roles in society.

More negative role models were identified in a parents' survey taken at the time of the penning of this book. Topping the list was former Disney star Miley Cyrus, who for years gave hope to parents as a wholesome character but changed into an R-rated performer without warning in August of 2013. And Chris Brown, the singer who assaulted Rihanna, had the distinct honor of being the top worst male role model.

Our government officials aren't much better. According to Emily Post, for proper etiquette our high-ranking government officials are to be addressed "The Honorable _____." However, with congressmen like Anthony Weiner with his sexting, former presidential candidate John Edwards's campaign finance fraud and infidelity, and Governor Mark Sanford skipping out of the country away from his family on Father's Day to be with a mistress, it is small wonder that our youth often have a difficult time finding their identities.

If sports stars and entertainers and even government officials are not the optimal role models, who should we be holding up as examples for society? A role model is someone whose life is worthy of emulation. Those would be individuals who not only are successful but who also contribute to the well-being of society at large. There is nothing that says these people need to be famous and many of the best role models live right in our own houses.

My Mother: One of the Best Role Models I've Seen

My mother provided for my brother and me a wonderful example of how not to be a victim. Even though the odds sometimes seemed stacked against her, she would never give up. I remember when my brother started high school they placed him in the vocational track instead of the college prep track. My mother was more than a little upset and ruffled many feathers from the local school all the way to the Board of Education of Detroit to alter that situation. I remember another time when a hit-and-run driver hit her car and sped away. She backed up the car and chased him for thirty minutes through the streets of Southwest Detroit before he finally gave up. You certainly did not have to worry about whether she could defend herself physically if she caught him, even though she was only five foot three. The example of tenacity and courage that she presented certainly was not lost on me and is a large part of who I am today.

Teachers as Role Models

Even though my mother was a terrific role model, she did not have the wherewithal to be a good academic mentor. Fortunately, I had several teachers along the way who recognized some potential in a poor boy from the ghetto, and decided to invest much time and effort to make sure that I not only mastered my school work but also listened to quite a bit of advice they gave me about how to be successful in life. I was particularly grateful for all the tips I received about college life and how to overcome the challenges it would present. Teachers frequently get a bad rap, but good ones can mean the difference between success and failure in many lives. When they are driven by their inherent goodness rather than some of the teacher unions, their potential for doing good is almost unlimited.

The Inventor as Role Model

When it comes to making contributions to society, inventors can serve as spectacular role models. People like Thomas Edison, Henry Ford, and Elijah McCoy, an inventor of locomotive lubrication systems, had profound effects on the way we all live. African American Garrett Morgan, widely known for his innovations with the traffic light, in 1916 demonstrated the effectiveness of his invention the "Morgan Safety Hood and Smoke Protector" (now known as the gas mask) by rescuing 32 men trapped 250 feet underground in a tunnel. Prior to that event, people had scoffed at his lifesaving innovation. This invention was then utilized by the U.S. Army, saving many lives during World War I, and is now commonly used all over the world by fire and police departments, as well as the military (http://inventors.about.com/od/mstartinventors/a/Garrett_Morgan.htm). Thomas Edison was a determined inventor who knew 999 ways a lightbulb did *not* work. His associate, Lewis Latimer, who came up with the filament that made the bulb last for more than a few days, happened to be born in Massachusetts of escaped slaves from Virginia. Although his parents had escaped six years before Lewis was born, he was still considered a slave and his freedom had to be defended by Frederick Douglass and William Lloyd Garrison in

Boston, actually purchasing his freedom himself, with the help of a local minister. After serving in the navy during the Civil War (he enlisted at age sixteen), he was honorably discharged.

Identifying Contemporary Role Models

All the people mentioned above embody the "can-do" attitude that helped America rapidly gain power and position in the world. Unfortunately, in the current atmosphere of division and demonization of political opponents and with the ever-present influence of political correctness, it is very difficult to identify generally admired people. But it is fair to say that most people admire courage and the willingness to sacrifice in order to achieve a goal. This is why people like Albert Einstein, Winston Churchill, Ronald Reagan, and John F. Kennedy are widely admired. They all had their flaws, as is the case with every one of us, but they all faced gigantic obstacles and were victorious. People like Helen Keller, Neil Armstrong, and many war heroes also demonstrated a level of courage that most of us can only dream about. Courage is admired so much because it is lacking in so many. People of courage tend to be much less concerned about their status with other people than they are with their ability to consistently uphold principles and values. Such people frequently are not appreciated during their lifetimes, but the pages of history are frequently kind to them. It takes some degree of wisdom to be able to identify the courageous role models living and working before our very eyes.

Action Steps

1. Discuss heroes and role models with the young people in your life. Ask who their role models are and recommend role models discussed in this chapter.
2. Discuss heroes and role models with the older people in your life and compare their answers with those of the young people. Are their role models similar or different?
3. Thank one of your role models for his or her example.
4. Examine your life. Could you be a role model for a younger person?

16

THE ORIGIN OF MORALITY

Those who follow the right path fear the Lord; those who
take the wrong path despise Him.

PROVERBS 14:2

When I was in my early teens, my brother and I acquired a BB
gun. We were excited and began shooting it behind the house,
using cans as targets. We were having so much fun that we
didn't think about where the errant BBs were going. The man
who lived across the alley came to our home holding a screen
with multiple holes in it. It looked amazingly like holes that
would be made by a BB gun. We didn't have money to replace
the screen, but agreed to do some chores for our neighbor.
Needless to say we stopped shooting the gun in the neighborhood.

However, our aunt Jean and uncle William lived out in the
country where there was plenty of space to shoot a BB gun and
we could hardly wait to get there. One Sunday morning while
we were spending the weekend with our relatives in the country, I spotted a red-winged blackbird that seemed to be an ex-

cellent target for an eagle-eyed BB gun marksman. I took careful aim at the beautiful creature sitting peacefully high above the fray in a tree. I really did not expect to hit the bird, but only seconds after I squeezed the trigger, the delicate form of the innocent creature fell lifelessly to the ground. I went over to the body and gazed at it with a combination of horror and pride. I was disgusted with myself for killing an innocent animal and I vowed never to shoot another bird and I never have.

Was I wrong to kill that bird and did it really even matter in the whole scheme of things? No one would really miss that bird except maybe the little chicks if this happened to be their mother out looking for food. Yet I couldn't find any way to assuage my guilt. The fact that I felt guilt obviously meant that I thought I had done something wrong—but how would I have known that? No one had ever explicitly told me not to shoot a bird, yet I had an innate sense that there was an absolute standard of morality that I had violated.

Who Says?

What is right? What is wrong? And who gets to determine the answers to these questions? For a nation to be truly united, most of its citizens must agree on the answers to these questions—or at least agree that there are answers to be found. For years, most Americans have turned to a belief in God and the Bible for answers. From the Creation story to the Ten Commandments to the Gospels to the Epistles, the Bible provided an explanation for the meaning of life and instructed us in moral principles. We held to a Judeo-Christian standard while respecting the beliefs of those who didn't share them, and that standard saved us from confusion. Today, fewer people believe in the Bible, or even in absolute truth, and our rejection of an objective moral standard has thrown our society into disarray. If in fact we do really believe in God and His word, many of the moral "gray" issues of today become black and white.

Abortion

According to God's word, life begins at conception rather than at the time of delivery or at some arbitrary point during gestation. Psalm 139:13-16 indicates that God knew the writer of these verses while he was yet unformed. In Jeremiah 1:4-5, there is an indication that God knew Jeremiah before he was born and had a special purpose for his life. This is one of several biblical passages that indicate a continuum of life that starts before birth and continues after death. In the Book of Exodus, chapter 21, verses 22–24, it is made quite clear that God considers the life of the unborn to be just as valuable as the life of an adult. When you couple this belief with the commandment, "Thou shalt not kill" (Exodus 20:13), it is clear that abortion is rarely a moral option. Add the commandment to "Love your neighbor as yourself" (Matthew 22:39), and it becomes clear that we ought to help care for mothers put in a tough place by unwanted pregnancies.

Recently I visited a place called the Hope Center in Greenville, Tennessee, where young women with unplanned pregnancies are nurtured, mentored, and encouraged to give birth whether or not they plan to keep the baby. They make provisions for adoption if the young woman chooses not to keep the child and provide resources and support if she wants to keep the baby. They also facilitate continued education and job training for these young mothers. The center is run by a Christian organization and they are doing exactly what they should be doing. We all need to be proactive in terms of providing solutions for those in our society who have made mistakes, rather than just criticizing them. This is what it means to be truly moral people.

Homosexuality

Another sticky moral issue is the topic of homosexuality. Many people do not understand why Christians object so strongly to gay marriage, but the answers are simply laid out in Scripture. First, several Bible verses reveal God's disapproval of homosexual behavior. For example, Leviticus 20:13 states, "If a man practices homosexuality, having sex with another man as with a woman, both men have committed a detestable act. They must both be put to death, for they are guilty of a capital offense." Jude 7, in the New Testament, says, "And don't forget the cities of Sodom and Gomorrah and their neighboring towns, which were filled with sexual immorality and every kind of sexual perversion. Those cities were destroyed by fire and are a warning of the eternal fire of God's judgment." Second, in Ephesians 5:31-32, Paul wrote, "As the Scriptures say, 'A man leaves his father and mother and is joined to his wife and the two are united into one.' This is a great mystery, but it is an illustration of the way Christ and the church are one." When you see that the Bible compares God's relationship with the church to the relationship between a man and a woman in covenant marriage, it is easy to see why those who believe that marriage is an institution established by God might be less than enthusiastic about changing the definition of that institution. Some Christians may interpret the Scripture differently, but the text remains fairly clear: Condoning homosexual behavior goes directly against God's commands. Changing the definition of marriage distorts God's illustration of His relationship with us.

This is not to say that God does not love homosexuals, because He most certainly does, just as He loves everyone regardless of their behavior. And Jesus died to pay the price for the shortcomings of everyone. Since there are no perfect people, no one but God has the right to judge our lives outside of criminal activity. Only He knows the minute details of every life from conception to death and can judge matters of the heart.

However, this does not mean that we have to accept man-imposed changes to God's word. We all make choices in life. In this matter, one can choose God's word or the gay marriage agenda. Even though the two are not compatible, people on opposite sides of the issue do not need to be hateful toward the other side. It also should be made quite clear that upholding traditional marriage does not mean that one is a homophobe. It appears almost impossible for the gay community to understand this last point. Whether they understand it or not, it is the job of the Christian community to love everyone as God loves us.

Evolution

Standing somewhat opposed to traditional morality is another form of religion, although its believers would never admit it. This religious belief is the theory of evolution. In this belief system, only the strong survive and there are no moral implications associated with the actions necessary to survive and thrive. As I have stated and written publicly, it might be more difficult for evolutionists to describe the basis of morality than it would be for a creationist.

This is not to say that those who believe in evolution have no morals, but I was attacked by some biology professors at Emory University in Atlanta for allegedly saying that evolutionists were unethical. I suspected that their real objective was to drum up support for their opposition to my being invited as the commencement speaker at Emory, since I was a creationist and they didn't think that such people had the right to be honored at an institution of higher learning. They started a petition and received many signatures, but a counterpetition received more than four times as many signatures.

I did speak at the commencement and was received very warmly, probably to the chagrin of the intolerant instigators, one of whom subsequently sent me a note of apology stating that they had misinterpreted what I said. Obviously I was not attacking the character of evolutionists, but as is so often the case, many people who disagree with your beliefs find it more convenient to distort them than to refute them, so they can proclaim you to be an idiot.

It is amusing to me that many in the "intellectual community" suggest that those with deeply held religious beliefs are antiscience. Many times I have heard it said of me that my opinions should not be held in high regard, because I believe that God created the earth six thousand years ago. How can anyone, they argue, with such beliefs understand anything about science and medicine, which is based on science.

I can unequivocally state that I love science and understand

and accept its basic laws. I do not know whether the earth is six thousand years old or not, and I'm not sure that such knowledge is important. The Bible says "In the beginning, God created the heavens and the earth." It then goes on to describe the creation week without in any way indicating what the period of time was that elapsed between the first verse of the Bible and the start of creation week. It could have been billions of years, or it could have been less than one day. That means the earth could be billions of years old, or it could have been created in an already mature state by God six thousand years ago.

To say that anyone believing this is stupid and nonscientific is pure demagoguery and bigotry, and certainly is uncharacteristic of a true scientist. The fact that I and millions of others believe that God created the earth and everything on it in an orderly fashion is no more antiscience than believing that something came from nothing, exploded and formed a perfectly organized solar system and universe, particularly in light of the second law of thermodynamics, which states that things tend to move toward a state of disorder. Both beliefs require faith in things that have not been proven and neither has the right to proclaim the other as foolish.

As a doctor, I have to say that it also requires a great deal of faith to believe that an organ system as complex as the kidney or the eye formed through the process of natural selection, which states that things that are not useful to an organ simply disappear, whereas things that are useful are genetically passed on to the next generation. There are many components to organs like the kidney or the eye that are useless without all the other components and, therefore, according to the theory of evolution, should not be passed on to the next generation. In fact, according to the theory of evolution, without invoking all kinds of convolutions to the theory, it is impossible for any complex organ system to exist unless it just spontaneously formed overnight. That sounds crazy to me, but then again, if you believe that matter can form from nonmatter, I guess you can believe an eyeball can form overnight.

My understanding of science has not precluded my pursuit of a career as a successful neurosurgeon. The claims of some in the scientific community that belief in the theory of evolution is the foundation of all science is pure and unadulterated fantasy. Belief in evolution is just as much associated with religion as belief in creation. They both require faith, either in God or in man.

Unlike godly principles that are uniting in nature, many who believe in the evolutionary approach drive wedges between people by insisting that all intelligent people believe as they do and that anyone with a different belief leaves something to be desired intellectually.

An interesting question that frequently arises during these kinds of discussions is whether or not animals are capable of distinguishing right from wrong. Is it wrong for a lion to kill an innocent lamb or even to kill a human being when it is hungry or even when it is just being a vicious killer? If evolutionary theory is true, nothing should separate humans from animals.

Yet, surprisingly, these kinds of questions are much easier to answer when we are dealing with people as opposed to animals. Unlike animals, we have gigantic frontal lobes in our brains that allow us to extract information from the past and the present, and then formulate a plan that can be projected into the future to guide our actions. We do not simply have to react to the environment, but can actually alter the environment to satisfy our needs. We have reasoning abilities that far exceed those of animals and our behavior, once we mature, is generally based on choices. Some may say that this impressive ability evolved, but I prefer to think we were given it on purpose. Either way, human beings have a sense of morality that does not jibe with evolutionary theory. It is legitimate to ask the question, "Where did our sense of morality come from?" Even if you enter the deepest, darkest jungles of Borneo, you will find that a thief tends to ply his trade in the darkness, when there is no one around to see him. This is even the case when there have been no missionaries in the area and no Bible to read. All people inherently seem to understand some basic principles of right and wrong. It is much easier to see such morality as God given than trying to explain how it evolved. But everyone is entitled to their beliefs.

Have you ever noticed how difficult it is to sit by and watch someone suffer? Almost everyone will try to help someone who is drowning. That might mean jumping into the water to save her, throwing her a lifesaver, trying to reach her with a pole, or calling for help. As a human being, this is your duty, because you certainly would want someone to do that for you. As an evolutionist who is also an atheist, your "survival-of-the-fittest" mentality should lead you to just walk on by, but of course your deep-seated humanity would not allow such callous behavior in most cases.

So where does that deep-seated humanity come from? Where did my conviction that wantonly killing an innocent bird was wrong come from? Has it evolved, or is it possible that if we are made in the image of God, there is an innate sense of right and wrong that we all share as human beings? I believe there is good evidence for the latter.

There are no people anywhere that I know of who don't have a sense of right and wrong. Even a cursory reading of the Bible demonstrates that people certainly knew the difference between right and wrong before the time of the Ten Commandments. It was the outrageous behavior of the Israelites that necessitated the physical writing out of a behavioral code, despite the powerful evidences of God in their lives.

I do not believe it to be necessary for us to all agree on the source of morality as long as we agree on the basic principles of what is right and what is wrong. I believe there is general agreement that lying, stealing, and murdering are wrong. There is probably less agreement about what constitutes adultery and whether it is wrong, especially in the nonchurch community. Nevertheless, our guiding principle should be to help rather than harm our fellow man. Doing so earns God's blessing.

Are We "Under God"?

In America we claim to believe in God and in fact proclaim our trust in Him on every piece of our money. Many of our laws are based on the Ten Commandments, and in the bas relief crown molding that adorns the principal chamber of the U.S. Supreme Court, Moses and the tablets containing the Ten Commandments are depicted. Yet we take great pains to delete references to God and the Bible from all public spaces, especially our schools and municipal buildings. We seem to be having a difficult time determining whether we actually believe in

God or whether it is something that we have gotten used to saying in a pro forma manner without actually thinking about our words.

The words *under God* were not in the original version of the Pledge of Allegiance. They were subsequently added to signify the importance of God in every aspect of our lives. Admittedly, the acknowledgment of God in virtually everything we do does not show a great deal of respect for atheists and others who do not harbor traditional views of God, but as the Bible says, you cannot serve both God and man. This does not mean we must force others to believe what we do, but it does mean we have to make a choice as to what we believe and form our societal values around that choice.

In no way does choosing God mean that we need to be unkind to nonbelievers. It is contrary to the American way to force our beliefs on anyone else. By the same token, it is most unreasonable for atheists to make attempts to legally force Christians and their beliefs underground. The persistent attempts by some atheist groups to have the words *under God* removed from our pledge or the phrase "In God we trust" removed from our money should be tolerated because we believe in being fair to everyone, but it is the height of absurdity to seriously consider such challenges in a country where religious freedom and freedom of worship are guaranteed.

Interestingly enough, we in the United States have had many manifestations of God's mercy and favor throughout history. In August of 1776, General George Washington and eight thousand troops were trapped on Long Island with British General Howe preparing to crush them the next morning. The island was surrounded by the British armada. Desperately, Washington drafted every local seaworthy vessel available, from fishing boats to rowboats, in an attempt to ferry his army across the East River all through the night. At dawn, many of his troops were still in grave danger by their exposure to the huge British fleet. However, most curiously, the fog that usually would rise from the river once the sun rose, did not move. It remained dense long enough for all of Washington's men to escape to safety. This had been the British's best opportunity to clinch the victory over the Americans. Major Ben Tallmadge, who was Washington's chief of intelligence, wrote of that morning:

As the dawn of the next day approached, those of us who remained in the trenches became very anxious for our own safety, and when the dawn appeared there were several regiments still on duty. At this time a very dense fog began to rise [out of the ground and off the river], and it seemed to settle in a peculiar manner over both encampments. I recollect this peculiar providential occurrence perfectly well, and so very dense was the atmosphere that I could scarcely discern a man at six yards distance . . . we tarried until the sun had risen, but the fog remained as dense as ever.

Like the Israelites in the Bible, we have wandered away from our strong belief in God and many of us now don't seem to know what we believe. Church attendance is steadily declining, especially among the millennials; traditional families are rapidly becoming a rarity; and many of the things forbidden by God are spreading like wildfire. Traditionally, once a nation starts down the path of lack of identity and vision for the future, it is destroyed, or deteriorates from within, losing most or all of its relevance to the world.

Although we appear to be sliding downward, it is possible for us to reverse the trend, even though we are composed of many people with lots of different ideas about morality. It may be hard to agree on the origin of morality but it should not be hard to agree that that sense of morality, should guide our decision making and determine what kind of society we have. As human beings we have a strong sense of right and wrong. As Americans, we have a heritage of Judeo-Christian morality. Let's remember who we are and unite around the vision dictated by our identity.

Action Steps

1. Ask your associates whether they believe absolute right or wrong exists.
2. Ask your friends whether they would be okay with polygamy if most people said it was okay with them.
3. Determine the basis for your moral code. Ask your friends how they have determined theirs.
4. If you believe God to be the author of morality, consider how you can better cultivate a relationship with Him.

17

TAKE COURAGE

Those who fear the Lord are secure; He will be a place of refuge for their children.

PROVERBS 14:26

The power of a determined human being who is not willing to give up is truly inspirational. I have been inspired over the years by many of my patients who have had absolutely devastating diseases. One young lady has endured over one hundred operations and was near death on many occasions, but persevered and graduated from high school in June 2013. Another patient, Mandy, who is well into adulthood now, has faced death on numerous occasions while remaining cheerful, upbeat, and unafraid. She is wheelchair bound and has significant weakness of the upper extremities along with other serious issues, but she will never give up, and even completed a college degree.

The question is do the people of this nation have the determination, drive, and willpower to seize the reins of power and return the country to its place as a beacon of light and inspiration for the world? A nation that is powerful, yet benign? Do

we have the courage to stand up for what we believe or will we continue to cower in the corner and hope no one sees us?

One way to develop courage is to consider what will happen if we fail to act. When considering action, I always do a best/worst analysis. I ask the following four questions about the prospective action:

1. What's the best thing that happens if I do it?
2. What's the worst thing that happens if I do it?
3. What's the best thing that happens if I don't do it?
4. What's the worst thing that happens if I don't do it?

Let's consider these questions with respect to being courageous enough to go against the flow of political correctness and demand your constitutional rights. What is the best thing that happens if we refuse to abide by the dictates of political correctness? I believe that we could return to a nation that truly cherishes freedom of speech and freedom of expression. A nation where people are unafraid to express their opinions and beliefs and are eager to engage in intelligent and constructive conversations about their differences. A nation where we value even those with whom we disagree and work together to accomplish common goals.

What is the worst thing that happens if we oppose political correctness? I believe that every attempt would be made to silence those who oppose political correctness and to make examples of them to discourage others. World history demonstrates that it is very difficult to eradicate every single fighter for freedom.

What is the best thing that happens if we don't oppose political correctness? I believe we would achieve a very homogeneous society with little original thought but complete harmony. What is the worst thing that happens if we don't oppose political correctness? I believe we could see a dictatorship with brutal domination of any individual or group that opposes the leadership. The worst things that can happen if we don't take action are considerably worse than the worst things that can happen if we do take action. Therefore, we must take action.

This exercise guided me as I considered topics for the National Prayer Breakfast. As it turns out, one of the better outcomes was achieved, because I have encountered thousands of Americans who had given up on our country, and now are reinvigorated and ready to stand up for the freedoms that are guaranteed in our Constitution.

There is no freedom without bravery. As a society, are we free if we tolerate intimidation by government agencies like the IRS? Are we free if we allow the NSA to illegally search and seize our private documents without cause? Are we free if we allow the purveyors of political correctness to muzzle our thoughts and our speech? Are we free if we allow ourselves to be forcibly placed into an ill-conceived health care system that controls the most important thing we have: our lives? Are we free when our government controls every aspect of the business community and stifles the entrepreneurial spirit that built America? We are in the process of relinquishing the freedom that is America. Are we really brave if we allow all these things to occur and keep silent because we're afraid that someone will call us a name?

Freedom is not reserved for those unwilling to fight for it. When you see the American flag, think about George Washington, who fought alongside his men and led a ragtag bunch of militiamen to a victory over what was then the most powerful empire in the world. Remember Alexander Hamilton, who used his financial wizardry to establish a viable financial structure for a fledgling nation. Consider John Adams and Sam Adams, who were willing to give not only of their resources but also tirelessly of their efforts to establish an understandable legal foundation for our nation. Honor the millions of soldiers who fought and died to preserve our freedom when the world was threatened by tyranny. Revere Dr. Martin Luther King Jr. and his dream of a nation where people were judged by the content of their character and not by the color of their skin. Imitate Henry Ford and Dale Carnegie, who used their entrepreneurial talents not only to enrich themselves but to provide a mechanism to proliferate and empower the middle class in America.

Why did all of these people toil so relentlessly for an idea? It is because they had a dream of a nation that was different from any other; a nation where people could determine their own destiny and choose their lifestyle based on their own endeavors; a nation where people could choose how to disperse their own wealth after contributing a small, but reasonable amount of their resources to conduct the affairs of government. Through complacency, are we ready to throw away their ideas and the results of their labors?

Our nation was formed by men and women of tremendous courage. If we think about it, I'm sure that each of us can remember numerous brave individuals whom we have encountered throughout life. I am aware of a multitude of my physician colleagues who have stood on principle and faced expensive and embarrassing public malpractice suits when they could have simply settled the case in secret. These courageous individuals refused to be blamed for bad outcomes when they not only did nothing wrong but had gone the extra mile to try to ensure the patient's well-being. Each such fight will get us closer to badly needed tort reform in our country.

When I was in high school, it was not uncommon for some of the tougher boys to intimidate and control many of the teachers. I was in the marching band and the concert band led by Mr. Dee. He was a short but stocky young man who refused to yield to intimidation. One of the boys who was particularly brutal repeatedly challenged Mr. Dee's leadership and many verbal confrontations ensued. One day after a practice session, Mr. Dee publicly challenged the belligerent young man to back up his verbosity. The two of them remained in the band room after everyone had left and I never knew what actually happened, but I did notice that the troublemaker never challenged Mr. Dee again. This example of courage was not lost on all the other students and demonstrates how teachers can be an important influence on students even outside of their area of expertise.

I have seen numerous examples of courageous patients and families throughout my career. In one case a young family from the western half of our nation had been told that their infant boy had only six months to live after a biopsy at the university hospital proved consistent with a malignant brain stem tumor. With help they made their way to Johns Hopkins Hospital where I performed a series of operations that would have been considered futile by many. The family never lost faith and endured many hardships, but had the courage and fortitude to persist in their efforts to save their child. A few years ago I was giving a lecture at the university in the home state of that patient and I was approached after the lecture by a young man and his family. It turned out to be the same young man on whom I had operated when he was an infant and he was now a junior at the university and had no neurological deficits. I feel confident in saying that he would not have been alive without the courage and persistence of his family. There are plenty of courageous people out there who can inspire all of us to undertake difficult tasks in order to achieve a better future.

The next time you hear the national anthem, think about what it means: "Oh, say does that star-spangled banner yet wave / O'er the land of the free and the home of the brave?" We are still the home of the brave, and it is time for us to stand up and preserve our flag and our freedoms.

EPILOGUE

We all have a tendency to assume that our day-to-day routines will continue as usual without catastrophes. I certainly made that assumption on March 20, 2012.

I was driving to work and was one block away from the hospital, entering an intersection with the green light in my favor. Another driver ran the red light on the perpendicular street going sixty miles per hour. Our cars met in the intersection and the next thing I knew there were flashing lights, police, and medics all around. My air bags had deployed and my car was completely destroyed.

I was relieved as I examined myself and found only a few minor scrapes and abrasions, as well as some chest discomfort from the explosive force of the steering air bag. My cell phone was broken, but an officer lent me his phone so I could call my wife. I also called the operating room to let them know that I would be slightly delayed, but intended to get there in time to complete the operations that were scheduled that morning. I convinced the officials that I was okay, and one of the police officers pried open the trunk to retrieve my briefcase. He then drove me the rest of the way to the hospital, where I completed three operations without incident.

Since that experience, I have frequently thought about how lucky I was to have not been killed or seriously injured that day. I keep a picture of the mangled mass that used to be my car on my phone to remind me of how fleeting life can be. Tomorrow is not guaranteed to any of us, and if something needs to be done, it is usually best to just go ahead and do it, rather than engage in endless cogitation with no action.

If we are not an exceptional nation, we can quietly continue our slide into insignificance, but if this is the America of Washington, Franklin, Lincoln, Kennedy, Edison, Ford, King, and the millions who gave their lives for our freedom, then we must shake off the indifference that has gradually stolen our pride and our freedom and threatens the future of our children. We must exercise our duty as responsible and informed citizens and actively shape the nation we desire by investing time, resources, and energy into choosing appropriate leaders who share our vision. In some cases, we may even need to offer ourselves as candidates for public office.

Who knows what tomorrow holds for each of us and for our nation? We have no time to waste. Today is the day to act. Resolve to take one step toward helping our nation return to greatness. If we all do so, we cannot fail to remain "one nation, under God, indivisible, with liberty and justice for all."

The New Beginning

ACKNOWLEDGMENTS

Many thanks to those who made this book possible, including Sealy Yates, Adrian Zackheim, Bria Sandford, Will Weisser, Washington Speakers Bureau, Audrey Jones, Stephanie Marshall, my many medical colleagues and patients, Armstrong Williams, and Xavier Underwood.

INDEX